Date Due

NOV 22 75	NOV 13		
JUL 23 76	DEC 22 1984		
JAN 21 77	APR 6 1985		
NOV 17 78	APR 2 87		
1/28/79	NOV 30		
MAY 1 79	OCT 4 2		
NOV 21 79			
4/8/80	FEB 1		
MAY 21 80			
DEC 12 80			
JUN 26 1982			

TRAPPING

The Craft and Science of Catching Fur-Bearing Animals

TRAPPING

The Craft and Science of Catching
Fur-Bearing Animals

BY

HAROLD McCRACKEN

and

HARRY VAN CLEVE

Illustrated by
HOWARD L. HASTINGS

South Brunswick and New York:
A. S. Barnes and Company
London: Thomas Yoseloff Ltd

A.S. Barnes and Co., Inc.
Cranbury, New Jersey 08512

Thomas Yoseloff, Ltd
108 New Bond Street
London W1Y OQX, England

Twelfth printing, 1974

ISBN: 0-498-08272-5

Printed in the United States of America

INTRODUCTION

THIS book presents the knowledge and advice of both a naturalist and a professional trapper—with a wealth of information on all varieties of fur-bearing animals in all parts of North America. It covers the various methods of trapping, from the semi-tropical swamps and deserts of the Gulf Coast and Mexican border to the snow-bound mountains, forests and frozen wastes of the Arctic. Its principal purpose is to provide the trapper with a broad foundation for his work, which will enable him to catch more fur and make more money from what he catches. For the beginner it is designed to provide about everything in the way of trapping information and advice which can be gained from the printed page and to guide him toward learning what experience and practice alone can provide. For the professional trapper of long experience it will no doubt provide some things which may have been overlooked or not fully understood, as well as much to be compared in his own experience with the conditions and methods used by fellow trappers who work under circumstances extremely different from his own. It is also sure to provide interesting reading for those merely interested in wild life and the out-of-doors.

Men have been trapping fur-bearing animals for a very long time and a lot of fundamentals have been learned. The printed page can be a valuable guide, as a means of passing on information which otherwise might require years of experience in trial and error to learn. But it must be kept in mind that in many respects trapping is like playing a piano or a violin—you can't just be told how it's done, in words and diagrams, and then go right out and play a pretty tune. It takes practice, as well as knowledge, to do it right.

The natural history information contained in this book is by Harold McCracken, whose experience and knowledge of wild life covers the field from the swampy Everglades of southern Florida to the Arctic coast of Alaska. Few men alive today have had a more extensive or complete experience. For more than a quarter of a century he was consistently occupied in collecting specimens of big and small game for museums and in photographing all forms of wild life from opossums to Kodiak grizzlies. At the age of eighteen he spent an entire winter in charge of a fur-trading post in the northern interior of British Columbia. One of the expeditions which he led, for The American Museum of Natural History, was on the famous Schooner *Morrissey*, with Captain Bob Bartlett, who in 1909 took Admiral Peary to within walking distance of the North Pole; and they covered all of the western coast of Alaska and a considerable section of the Arctic coast of Siberia on this trip. All in all he has spent more than five years in Alaska and the Yukon, where he also was engaged in fox trapping, handling live foxes for propagation and fur-buying. He is one of our best known present-day writers of animal biographies; among which are such books as "The Last of the Sea Otters," "The Biggest Bear on Earth," "Sentinel of the Snow Peaks," "The Great White Buffalo," "Alaska Bear Trails," and others.

The practical trapping information in this book is based on the life-long experience and research of one of this country's foremost authorities on the subject. Probably no other living man has had a professional contact with more trappers, or had an opportunity to study and analyze trapping methods and problems on a broader scale than Harry Van Cleve. As Manager of the Trapper's Service Department of the Animal Trap Company of America, makers of the famous "Victor" and "Newhouse" traps, it has been his job to keep in touch with conditions and circumstances relating to all problems connected with professional trapping in every section of North America and to be a source of advice in helping thousands of professional trappers work out their most difficult problems. This responsibility has also extended into nearly every foreign country. And this book serves as the culmination of his long active career in this specialized field.

Harry Van Cleve began trapping in southern Fulton County, Pennsylvania in the early 1880's. He learned the hard way. For in those days, as in many cases today, it was customary for a successful trapper to keep his knowledge and methods strictly to himself. Any information which may have been passed along by him was generally misleading rather than helpful. But young Harry learned this trapping business well—so well in fact that in 1916 when the State of Pennsylvania was establishing its game refuges across the northern tier of counties, he was made a member of the Pennsylvania Game Commission, to use his extensive knowledge in the effort to safeguard and preserve the State's dwindling wild life. In 1920 he was engaged in what is considered one of the most outstanding game re-stocking projects on record—which resulted in the re-establishing of the beaver as a fur-bearer trapping industry in Pennsylvania. For twenty years, Van Cleve served the Pennsylvania Game Commission—as Refuge Keeper, County Game Protector, State Trapping Instructor on predatory animals, and in other responsible capacities, until he was retired in 1936 at the age of 65. It was after this that he was engaged by the Animal Trap Company to head their important trapper's service and information department.

These two authorities combine to make this book the most complete and comprehensive work of its kind ever published.

THE PUBLISHERS

CONTENTS

TRAPPING
The Craft and Science of Catching Fur-Bearing Animals

CHAPTER I

THE FIRST TRAPPERS

TRAPPING is one of the oldest occupations of man. It is older than agriculture and probably even preceded the pursuit of hunting and fishing. And yet, the manner by which the present day trapper goes about his task has changed but little since history began. Agriculture has been mechanized and in most every other respect made so different that primitive man could not possibly understand our modern farm. Methods of transportation have changed even more—from walking and carrying one's possessions on one's own back, we now travel at fantastic speeds by airplane. Think of the changes that have taken place in medicine, in communication, housing, warfare and practically everything that we do. But about the only thing that has been added to trapping, in thousands of years, has been the steel trap.

We seldom stop to realize that there was a time when the most up-to-date weapon our ancestors had at their disposal was a crude wooden pole, the end of which was merely given a sharp point by rubbing it on a piece of sandstone. That's all they had with which to protect themselves from the many large and dangerous animals which had not yet learned to fear man; and this pointed pole was the only weapon they had with which to fight their primitive battles. Even the bow and arrow had not yet been invented. But men and their families had already cultivated an appetite for meat, and a liking for clothing made from the skins and furs of animals. Some of the smaller animals they were able to catch in their hands, or kill with clubs or hurled stones; and they occasionally procured the flesh and skins of larger animals which had been killed in fights between themselves. Thus enters upon the scene the first trapper.

The first method of trapping animals was in pit-falls. For this, primitive man got his idea from observing how animals in mass migrations or stampede, fell over cliffs or became lodged in quick-sand. They found that a deep pit dug in the ground, along a trail or near a water-hole and carefully covered with a flimsy screen of sticks and grass or leaves, was capable of bringing the most ferocious animal under a control in which they could safely be killed with their sharp-pointed poles or hurled stones. Incidentally, many of the primitive tribes of today, in Africa, Asia and South America, still use this method, and it is sometimes even used by modern wild animal trappers—with practically no changes whatever since it was first devised at least 200,000 years ago.

The dead-fall and the snare followed the pit-fall in man's quest for more satisfactory methods in trapping. These too have very ancient origin, but not different in principle or application to their present day use.

With the skins of the animals which primitive man captured he learned to fashion many useful things. Not only did this provide food and clothing for himself and his family, but he began making shelters which could easily be transported from place to place, bedding, utensils of many kinds, as well as ropes, ornaments and scores of useful articles which soon became necessities of daily life. Thus trapping became one of the first and most important occupations of the human race; and thus began the development of man's culture, which has led to the airplane, the electric light and atomic energy.

When Europeans first visited North America this continent was more profusely populated with wild game and fur-bearing animals than any other part of the earth; and the nations were entirely dependent upon the most primitive means of trapping them. At that time the American Indians were living in a Stone Age—a state of existence which Europeans had outgrown many thousands of years before. The Indian's most highly developed implement was the bow and arrow; and the dead-fall and snare were their most effective methods of procuring both big and small game. The biggest bears were easily taken in dead-falls; and there was hardly an animal, large or small, which they could not take with their snares. We are told by the early historian Perrot that "the Ojibwa Indians snared no fewer than 2,400 moose on the island of Manitoulin during the single winter of 1670-71." Caribou were also captured in much the same way, the animals "being driven among trees and poles planted at intervals, in which were stretched snares of rawhide." This same method was used by certain Indian tribes of California to snare elk as late as 1850.

The American Indians had learned to attach their snares to spring poles or small trees bent down and held by trigger-devices, which, when released by the caught animal jerked it into the air or otherwise aided in the general purpose for which the snare was intended. The spring-pole was often used in trapping fur-bearing animals, which would thus be suspended up in the air out of the reach of other animals that might otherwise destroy it before the Indian got there.

Sometimes the Indian would set his snare and hide a short distance away. A rattle made of a bunch of dried deer hoofs would be attached, the noise of which would tell when game had been caught and the trapper could return and kill it with arrow, spear or club. Sometimes the Indian's snares took the form of nets. Such a device was popular, until fairly recently, among the Indians of the Northwest, for trapping beaver. These were made of skin thongs, or *babiche* as the French called them. The net was generally about twelve feet in length by six feet deep, and made of about four-inch meshes. A draw-cord passed around through the outer meshes, which, when pulled, brought the net together into a closed bag. The net was set through a hole in the ice across the under-water path used by the beaver in leaving their den or lodge. The draw-string was attached to a pole, or sapling, to which was also attached a rattle. When all was prepared, the hunter would break into the beaver's house, and the fleeing animals becoming entangled in the meshes of the net would cause the rattle to sound, at which time the trapper would hurry to pull the draw-cord and drag the captured beavers out onto the ice. Under other circum-

stances, after setting the net the trapper would make a little camp
and lie down or even go to sleep, with the draw-cord tied around
his wrist—and wait until a pull against the net would awaken
him to complete the capture.

There were many forms of snares and the Indian had become
very clever in using them. There were snares devised to use on
land, in water and in the air; and they acted by tension, spring-
pole, gravity, hatchet, point, and, after the introduction of metal,
by fish-hook and blade.

The dead-fall and the various primitive forms of killing traps
were an advancement over the snare. Some of these were quite
complex, consisting of working parts and simple automatic
mechanisms for setting and release—entirely primitive and made
without the use of metal of any kind. In these cases the victim
generally caught himself, releasing the dead-fall or killing device
by stepping upon the trigger, rubbing against it or pulling at a
bait. The killing device generally consisted of a suitable sized log,
sometimes weighted down by additional logs, large boulders, or,
among the Eskimos, even great blocks of ice. These trapping devices were as varied and clever as the snares, and included means
of taking everything from weasel to bears.

There were also some ingenious though rather devilish devices
designed by the primitive trapper. Among these are the Eskimo
method of tightly wound or doubled-up sections of sharp whale
bone, enclosed in frozen fat; which was put out where bear or
wolf would find and swallow it. Once inside the animal's stomach
the skewer would be released when the fat melted, and cause
ultimate death. The Eskimos also practiced setting a very sharp-
edged flint or obsidian knife into the frozen ground over which
warm fat was poured. When a pack of wolves found the "set"
they licked the now frozen fat until their tongues were so cut
and bleeding that the smell of blood infuriated the whole pack
and drove them to kill one another.

There were also the pen-traps, which were a development of the
pit-falls. These were at first simply stockades into which game was
driven. Some were, however, of great size covering the equivalent
of many acres or even square miles; with wide "wings" which

converged into a compound, large pit, or at the brink of a steep cliff, and required the service of whole villages.

It would require a whole book to describe all of the primitive methods of trapping used by our American Indians alone. But the most important factor in the whole story is the Indian's intimate knowledge of the game he sought to trap. From early childhood he devoted a goodly part of his attention to seriously observing and studying the wild animals around him. Their every habit and peculiarity was well known to him and this was the real secret of his success.

Many millions of very clever men have devoted a goodly part of their lives, thought and ingenuity to trapping; and yet, the only practical contribution which all our modern mechanical genius has made to this oldest of man's professions, is the comparatively simple steel trap. There have been a few mechanical gadgets put on the market from time to time, but it is the simple old steel trap, and it alone, which meets the requirements of the most successful trappers of today.

Just who first "invented" the steel trap is not known.

Probably the earliest known records of metal spring traps are those which were employed for the catching of human beings. These man-traps were in use in England about 1750 or a little thereafter. In general appearance and principle of operation they are fundamentally the same as those used today, although in size these man-traps were as much as six feet and two inches in length and weighed eighty-eight pounds. The jaws were correspondingly heavy and set with pointed teeth a full inch and a half in length. Their strength was sufficient to instantly break the bones in any man's leg. They were set in much the same fashion of today and their intended human victims were the poachers who trespassed in private forests and other such places where game was to be found but not permitted to be hunted by the general public. Use of such traps was permitted by the English laws, which also specified that adequate signs must be posted by the owners or proprietors as a warning to poachers that the traps were hidden in the area. This seems to be the origin of the present day custom of "posted" hunting grounds. Several examples of these man-traps are in the British

Museum—and it is singularly interesting to notice their similarity to traps now used for the capture of fur-bearing animals.

The history of the steel trap as an industrial product made available to trappers of fur-bearing animals, begins in 1823, in the village of Oneida Castle, near the Oneida Indian Reservation in central New York, and it has to do with the story of a young man by the name of Sewell Newhouse. His taste was all for hunting and the rough life of the woods. His genius was mechanical. His father had a blacksmith shop wherein young Sewell made traps and guns for his own use, which were the marvel of his neighbors and the envy of every Indian for miles around. The springs of the traps were made from worn out scythes, old axe blades and old files. The bottoms and crosspieces were made from blacksmith's scrap. Sewell had his share of Yankee shrewdness. He cultivated the friendship of the Indians, and with it, a very substantial trade in traps, which were usually exchanged for valuable furs.

When the followers of the religious organization Oneida Community moved to the banks of the Oneida Creek (where it bought a portion of the recently opened Indian Reservation), young Newhouse became a convert and joined. In 1848 and 1849 the Oneida Community was very poor. The members were practical men and women—New England farmers, shopkeepers and mechanics— and, having proved to their own satisfaction that farming alone offered a very precarious support, they resolved to turn a part of their labor to some mechanical industry. That was the beginning of their trap business.

By that time Newhouse was already supplying many hundreds of dozens of traps to the trade and often had two helpers in his shop at Oneida Castle. A small shop was now erected on Community property, for trap making, and Community men, women and even children, outside of their school hours, worked enthusiastically together, making up whatever traps they could sell. Mr. Newhouse superintended everything. Crude and clumsy as these old traps of the 40's and 50's look now, they were far ahead of anything to be obtained at that time, and were perfectly reliable. At first they were made by hand, even the springs being forged out with hammer and anvil. Later, trip-hammers and special machines were introduced.

After satisfying the local requirements, sales came very slowly. Steel traps were then practically unknown to trappers, and the demand had to be created. One of the men of the Community happened to be going to Chicago and took two trunks filled with traps, which he sold so readily to hardware firms there, that he returned to Oneida for more . . . and thus the trap manufacturing business began to spread.

In 1854, a machine shop was moved from Newark, N. J., to Oneida, and traps were first manufactured on a larger scale. The first traps were all of small size—No. 1; but Sewell Newhouse and John Hutchins now designed the larger sizes—first No. 4, for beaver; then No. 3 for otter, No. 2 for fox, No. 1½ for mink, and No. 5 for bear; later No. 0 and No. 6 were made. With these sizes and the introduction of special machinery, the business expanded until it outgrew its quarters in the old "Mill"; and the organization which Sewell Newhouse began has undergone numerous enlargements and changes through the years. Today it is known as the Animal Trap Company of America and has a spacious plant at Lititz, Pennsylvania. Perfections have been made in the manufacture and the metals used in making traps; but the principle remains quite the same. There are, of course, other manufacturers of steel traps; but their products are based upon the same fundamental principle utilized by the original Sewell Newhouse.

CHAPTER II

DRAMA AND DOLLARS IN FURS

THE FUR INDUSTRY has always been one of drama and dollars. Going back along the parade of years of the fur trade, we find a wealth of adventurous and historic lore which is unexcelled by any other pursuit of man. In many important instances the fur trade has shaped the course of empires and history. All Canada might today be a province of France, if it had not been for the furs which caused the British to establish themselves on Hudson's Bay in 1670, and for 93 years to wage the strenuous struggle which resulted in their becoming our northern national neighbor, instead of the French. It was sea otter skins which caused the Russians to settle and gain control of Alaska—otherwise that rich territory would most likely have become a part of Canada and never a possession of the United States. The fur trade was the purpose which sent Pierre Radisson to blaze the first white man's trail from the Great Lakes to the Upper Mississippi; and in 1721 sent Charlevoix from Quebec down the Mississippi to New Orleans and to make the French rulers of the vast Louisiana Territory; and sent other Frenchmen pushing boldly westward to the Missouri, even to the Rockies and the headwaters of the Saskatchewan—long before our Revolutionary War. It was also the fur trade which was the fundamental purpose behind the famous Lewis and Clark Expedition, and our establishing claim and con-

trol over the whole northwestern part of what is now the U.S.A.
These are but a few of the many instances in which the fur trade
provided the greatest single factor in the exploration, development
and destiny of North America.

The early history of our great West is replete with the names
of trappers, whose personal stories will endure as long as we are
a nation. Books have been written about their adventures and
monuments erected to commemorate their historic accomplishments. It was those solitary trappers who really "discovered,"
explored and laid the foundation for this great land of ours. To
those buckskin-clad adventurers, who rolled back the wilderness
and planted the seeds of the great civilization which followed,
this nation owes undying credit and honor. Defying death in their
bitter feud with the Indians, and enduring the worst of human
hardships, it was the trappers who crossed the unmapped plains
in every direction; traced the unnamed streams to their sources;
found the passes through the mountains; and pointed the way for
Government explorers to whom history has unfortunately given
undue credit for the accomplishments. It was the camping places
of the early trappers which became the sites for ranches, farms
and present-day towns; their trails became the routes for our
paved highways and streamlined railways; and their trading posts
became the big cities and industrial centers of the richest and
most powerful nation on all the earth. No chapter in the history
of this or any other country is more colorful, exciting or dra-
matic; and no contribution has been more important. No class of
pioneer empire-builders were ever more hardy, fearless, or more
skillful in frontier ways.

From the Alleghenies to the Pacific slopes of the Rockies, and
from the Frozen Sea and the bleak Barren Lands to Mexico and
the swamps of the Mississippi delta, the pioneer trappers penetrated every section of the vast wilderness. Into the lands of the
Shoshones and Snakes, the Cheyennes and Comanches, the Pawn-
ees, Utes, Crees, Apaches, and all the rest, they went.

Into the deep woods and bleak Barren Lands of the North they
went by birch-bark canoes and sleds, made with their own hands;
carrying provisions and traps. They made their own snow shoes,
webbed with the skin of moose they killed. They traveled light,

with the barest of life's necessities; enduring the bitter cold; and generally spending the long winters alone.

In the wide expanse of virgin country farther south, the trapper traveled by horse as well as canoe. Here the weather was not so severe, but the constant menace of Indians more than made up for that. In the most perilous regions he frequently was compelled to travel after night-fall, paddling silently along the streams in the shadow of the trees or the bank. The handle of his paddle was muffled where it might strike the gunwale. Sometimes he slipped past in sight of weird figures silhouetted against the flames of a big camp fire, where the Indians were celebrating their scalp dance. Frequently he moored his canoe in mid-stream, carefully hidden among big jams of driftwood, to catch a little sleep; for if he went ashore to roll up in his buffalo robe, a tomahawk or arrow might abruptly end his slumber.

It must be emphasized, however, that the white trapper was a trespasser in a land that had been the home of the red men from time immemorial. At the beginning the Indian had welcomed the white man with hospitality; but many a sad experience had convinced the Indian that he faced an invasion which was depriving him of the things he held most dear . . . and it would have been to his everlasting discredit if he had not fought desperately for what was rightfully his. Thus began one of the most bitter feuds in the history of nations.

Even when on his trapping ground, the white trapper did not always take the trouble to build a camp or a fire, except in very cold weather. A couple of deer or buffalo skins stretched over a willow frame was usually all he had for the worst that might come his way. Sometimes it was only a blanket or a buffalo robe in which he rolled up on the ground in the shelter of a rocky cliff or the bank of a ravine.

The trapper's few possessions were of vital importance. His powder horn and bullet pouch, when not in use, were carefully protected by the skins of the animals he caught. His rifle was always kept in condition and within handy reach. His horse or horses were well hobbled and never permitted to roam out of sight; for to be left stranded afoot by horse-stealing Indians was a real disaster.

The old-time trapper's habits and character often became as simple, primitive and fierce as the other creatures around him. This was often necessary to survive. Being a keen observer of nature and wild life was fundamental to success. They rivaled the beasts of prey and the stealthy Indian in skill and cunning. Constantly exposed to perils of all kinds, they became hardy as bears; wary as antelope; callous as wolves; and made the staunchest of friends and the most bitter of enemies.

The Indian was their greatest hazard. Some of them became friendly with the tribes in whose country they trapped, and even married squaws, but as a whole they were bitter enemies. This may not have been the Indian's fault . . . but the fact remained the same. Sometimes a redskin would set his determination for the scalp of a particular trapper, and follow him for days, like a mountain lion on the trail of an elk. He would watch the white man set his traps on some timbered stream that was suitable for the devilish purpose. Then crawling up through the water, so as to leave no signs of his presence, he would lie in ambush and wait for the trapper's return to examine his traps. Sometimes the trapper had already become suspicious, and would slip back by an unexpected route, to outwit the Indian by his own superior method of still hunting. But often . . . whizz! flew an arrow, which at such close range seldom failed to strike its designated mark. This was the real price of fur in those adventurous days. But for one scalp that dangled in the smoke of an Indian's lodge or was paraded proudly in the dances about the camp fires, a dozen black ones theoretically ornamented the trading posts and their story-telling confabs when the trappers gathered at the end of the season.

It was always a gala occasion when the trappers came in with their horses or their canoes heavily loaded with furs. The traders waited at pre-arranged rendezvous and trading posts, with plenty of money and goods to exchange The goods had to be transported long distances on river boats or by wagon train across the plains. These loads of supplies were particularly rich prizes for the Indian war parties; and for these reasons the prices were always high to the legitimate buyer. But the trappers invariably had lots of fur and were in a hearty mood for spending. Relaxation and let-down from the long ordeal of danger and hardship was often expressed with intensity. The gathering places generally became the scene of wild events. But there were also those who took life and the future more seriously; carefully saved their profits; and as the years passed and civilization slowly followed in their tracks, gained control of large tracts of the fertile land or in other ways laid the foundations for the substantial and prosperous generations who have since descended from them.

Names such as Daniel Boone, Kit Carson, Jedediah Smith, Bill Williams, Major Andrew Henry, William Ashley, Peter Skene Ogden and a host of others, should be boldly engraved in our national history.

Most of these men were "lone wolves," who had no desire for fame or glory. Much has been written about some of them; but in most instances a large part of their stories has been lost for the record, because of their life-time reluctance or refusal to even talk about their own thrilling careers.

Let's take a very brief glance at what a few of these early trappers did. Of all of them there is none more deserving of lasting fame than Daniel Boone—who has come to be a sort of legendary patron saint to all outdoorsmen, young and old—and he was all that his name implies. He was born July 14, 1732, at Exeter, Pennsylvania, about 60 miles from Philadelphia. His father was a farmer, none too prosperous, with seven sons and four daughters. When still in his teens, young Dan was supplying the large Boone family with wild game for food; and he spent his winters trapping as a means of supplying funds for the family maintenance. When Dan was 18 they moved to North Carolina, about ten miles from the present town of Wickersborough. This was pretty wild country in those days, and here hunting and trapping became Dan's chosen profession. He spent the most of his time on long trips in the forest and invariably traveled alone. He was a most ardent student of every variety of wild animal—which study he pursued until he knew practically every detail of their habits and life history. In his later years, if Daniel Boone had written a natural history, it would undoubtedly be today one of the outstanding authorities on the subject.

It was in 1760 that Daniel Boone made his first trip westward through the Cumberland Gap into the wild and little explored country which the Indians called "Kentucky" and the white men came to know as the "dark and bloody ground." It was in this country that he won his immortal fame as a master backwoodsman, and his historic title as the founder of the State of Kentucky.

There were six in that original party, all of whom were soon killed by Indians, except Daniel Boone. But so rich was the country in fur and so much did he love its wild forests, that he remained alone for the balance of two years.

Later, with his family and a group whom he induced to go with him, he built a fort on the bank of the Kentucky River, which was named Boonesborough. Two of his sons were killed in fierce fights with Indians; his fourteen-year-old daughter was captured and sensationally rescued from the raiding red men; and Daniel Boone himself was finally captured by the Shawanees, who took their human prize to their own principal village of Chillicothe on the Little Miami, in what is now the State of Ohio. His courage, daring and wilderness cleverness was so wildly renowned even among the Indians that they not only did not torture him, but eventually inducted him into the tribe. He was given the Shawanee name "Sheltowee" ("Big Turtle") and henceforth considered as the adopted son of the mighty war chief Blackfish. After more than six months however, he escaped and got back to Boonesborough.

Daniel Boone's wilderness adventures are legion. He was fundamentally a hunter and trapper. His exploits against the Indians were incidental necessities for the preservation of himself, his family and fellow pioneers. To combat the menace and repeated attacks by Indians, each district formed its own regiment of armed fighters, and Daniel Boone was made Lieutenant Colonel of his regiment—during the "bloody year of 1782."

When Kentucky became a State of the Union in 1792, Daniel Boone lost title to all of his lands, due to petty technicalities of the colonial laws.

In 1795, saddened and in very difficult circumstances, Colonel Boone left Kentucky and returned to Virginia. He had outwitted and beaten the Indians, in all their wilderness methods; but he lost to the white men of the government he had helped to establish!

Shortly afterward, however, the Spanish Lieutenant Governor of Upper Louisiana offered the famous backwoodsman a large tract of land north of St. Louis, in what is now the State of Missouri, if he would settle there. This offer was accepted and in 1795 Daniel Boone, his wife and son Daniel, migrated to the new land in the further west. They were the first American citizens to settle within the present limits of Missouri.

This was then a hunter's and trapper's paradise. There was an abundance of deer, buffalo, bear, turkey, prairie chickens, quail, beaver, otter and other game and fur.

Twice each year, until he was well past 80, he made hunting and trapping expeditions into the wilderness. And even in his old age he preferred to go alone. Some of these trapping trips took him as far as the present State of Iowa; and it is by some claimed that he even went to the vicinity of Yellowstone Park—long before Lewis and Clark made their historic journey into the great Northwest.

He died on September 26, 1820, at 86.

Another trapper who won enduring and well deserved fame is Christopher (Kit) Carson. According to no less an authority than Buffalo Bill, he was "this country's most distinguished representative of the intrepid race of mountaineers, and its most noted trapper, guide, pioneer and Indian fighter. As a frontiersman, in all honorable characteristics, he had no superiors, if indeed his equal ever lived."

Kit Carson was born in Madison County, Kentucky, on December 24, 1809. The following year the family moved to Upper Louisiana, in what is now Howard County, Missouri.

Kit's father was extremely poor, having to spend a large part of his time hunting and trapping to supply the family with food and clothing. At a very early age Kit considerably relieved his father of these interesting duties, and became an exceptionally expert hunter and trapper. At 15, however, the family difficulties demanded a more profitable occupation, and he was apprenticed to a saddlemaker. But at 17 he deserted this apprenticeship and joined a band of traders bound over the Santa Fe Trail to the wild southwest. Thus began the adventurous career of the great Kit Carson, the "Monarch of the Plains."

After arrival at Santa Fe, Kit went to Fernandez de Taos, where he spent a year catching and breaking wild horses with a party of Mexicans engaged in this business. When he had saved sufficient money he joined a group of trappers who went to the Gila River, in Arizona, a country rich in fur but dangerous for white men because of hostile Indians. Here Kit won a reputation of outstanding courage, skill and rare presence of mind in the face of grave danger.

After trapping with much success in this district, Kit joined a small group bound on the perilous trip through the Rocky Mountains to the Sacramento Valley in Mexican controlled California. This trip was full of great hardships. While crossing the desert, the party was compelled to kill several of their horses, drinking the blood and eating the meat to save themselves from death for want of water and food. But the beautiful Sacramento Valley amply repaid the toil and hardship. They caught an abundance of beaver; and Kit Carson repeatedly distinguished himself as an Indian fighter and frontiersman of unusual qualities.

Before Kit Carson was 21 he had traveled, trapped, fought Indians and become a pathfinder through more sections of the wild West than most men who had spent a full life beyond the Mississippi; and even among the bravest and the toughest of the frontiersmen, he already held a place of enviable esteem. He learned to know the country and the Indians of the Platte, Sweet Water, Arkansas, Colorado, Great Salt Lake, Yellowstone, headwaters of the Missouri and a great deal more. He fell in love with a beautiful Comanche Indian girl, whom he married. They had a daughter, and the little girl's mother sacrificed her life for Kit Carson when he was taken ill.

In 1842, when General John C. Fremont organized the first of his famous Government expeditions to officially explore a route through the Rocky Mountains to California, he chose the long-haired Kit Carson as his chief guide. He also served as guide for Fremont's second and third expeditions, leading them through the Mexican controlled California and on up to Oregon. He also figured prominently in some of the most critical battles in the war which resulted in the vast California Territory becoming a part of the United States.

Although trapping was his principal occupation, in later years he was made a Colonel, in command of the 1st Regiment, New Mexico Volunteer Cavalry; and as Government Indian Agent for New Mexico, he helped to create the Indian Reservation System adopted by the U.S. Government, and devoted his last years to working out the difficulties with the Indians.

On May 23, 1868, while mounting a spirited horse, an artery in his neck was ruptured and he died in a few minutes. Kit Carson left behind a reputation of highest esteem among both white men and red men. He was a polished gentleman or the toughest of the plainsmen, as circumstances required; a reckless madcap in the face of greatest danger, but skillfully cautious whenever caution led to honorable safety.

The lives of these men, and the many others like them, who made early history throughout the great West, are an undying credit to their race and profession. There are hundreds of them who deserve a place in history. The names of some of them, who accomplished much, unfortunately mean but little to the average person today. For example, Jedediah Smith, the "fighting Methodist" trapper; "Old Bill" Williams, one of the most picturesque of all; Jim Bridger; etc., etc. The names of many of them are entirely lost. They all found high adventure and contributed their own important part to the future development of the land they helped to explore.

Many are the great American fortunes which had their beginning in the fur trade. Our first "millionaire" was among these. His little shop in lower New York City had a crude sign over its door that read: "Furs and Pianos." He was born in a small German village called Waldorf, from which he came to this country as a poor immigrant and got a job in one of the fur trading establishments at $2.00 a week and board. When he first started out for himself he wandered about New York City's trading section with a basket of trade goods under his arm, looking for people who had furs to trade. Then he started going into the country, traveling from farm to farm, in search of furs. Soon he was going as far as the Great Lakes. Within fifteen years he was worth $2,000,000.

Then in 1810 he sent a big fur trading expedition clear across the continent and established a trading post at the mouth of the Columbia River—which grew into what is now the great city of Astoria. Today one of the world's finest hotels, the famous Waldorf-Astoria, commemorates the name of that little German village and the poor boy who set out for America with a small bundle of clothing tied to the end of a stick. The fur trade made the name of John Jacob Astor one of the most glamorous in financial history.

It is this colorful and credible lore of the past that walks the silent trails with every trapper today, whether he tramps a hundred-mile-long trap line beyond the frontier of the far north, or has but a few small traps set within sight of the church spire of a small town in any farm community.

CHAPTER III

TODAY'S BUSINESS OF TRAPPING

TRAPPERS in the United States today collect annually an estimated $100,000,000 from the raw furs they catch. The in-
dustry as a whole amounts to about a billion dollars a year.
That's a lot of money; and the business which it involves con-
stitutes one of our important industries.

One of the most attractive things about trapping is that it does
not require any great amount of capital to start into business. The
"equipment" necessary for even a long trap line in the far north,
costs less than a milk-separator, a plow, or a peanut vending machine—and yet the trapper can make for himself several thousands
of dollars during a few weeks' interesting work. On the other
hand, many a good farmer has little fur-bearing animals running
around on his land, and entirely taking care of themselves, the
prime pelts of which are worth more in dollars and cents than he
can get for the best domestic stock he owns and which he has
spent a good many months of careful effort and considerable ex-
pense in raising. But the unfortunate part of the whole situation
is that far too many folks fail to look upon these fur-bearers and
trapping as a serious business. What farmer would let dogs chase
his sheep or his hogs to some unknown place; or would go out and
willfully try to kill every last one of his breeding stock? And yet
how many farmers and ranchers try to do just that with the

valuable fur-bearing animals on their land. If the land-owner will look upon the mink, beaver, skunk, muskrat and other fur-bearers that make their homes on his property, in much the same way he looks upon, protects and fosters the other live stock he possesses, he will have more money in the bank at the end of each year.

Farmers have been known to have "cleaned out" all the skunks on their place, in mid-summer when the hides were without value, merely because the "varmints" killed one of their chickens. It would have been more profitable, in many such cases, to have "cleaned out" the chickens and taken care of the skunks! And more than one farmer has drained a swampy area, or cleared a wooded section on his place, which would have proved more profitable to him if that land had been left as it was, or improved for the benefit of the fur bearers. In many instances it is better to put in a dam or two, and plant some feed, to make your waste land so attractive that the fur bearers will stay and thrive, rather than chase them away.

The remuneration from trapping, both in financial returns and the fascinating enjoyment of the great out-of-doors, does not necessitate one going deep into the wilds. The farmer and farmer boy who runs his trap line through the woods on his own place, or down through the nearby river bottom or foothills, sometimes gets as much out of it as the person who winters in a crude log cabin in the remoteness of the far northwest.

There are also many who through the circumstances of life are compelled to spend their days at a work bench or in an office building, but whose hearts are really in the winter woods. Many such persons have trap lines a considerable distance from the towns in which they work and which are reached a certain number of mornings or evenings each week by automobile. There are also others who work in town during the summers and spend the entire trapping season in the wilds.

The amount and value of fur caught by farmers and part time trappers throughout rural America runs into a fabulous total—and the health and real pleasure which these men and boys enjoy, is even greater.

It is sometimes surprising what wild sections may exist within reach of the town or even the city in which you live; and not all of the wilderness in the United States is in the far north or the far west. There are sections along the Eastern Shore, particularly in the Carolinas and Georgia, as well as the Appalachian and Adirondack Mountains, and the Gulf Coast, which are but seldom visited and are about as wild as anyone might hope to find. In some of these sections the native white inhabitants have been isolated so long that they still retain customs and speak dialects of hundreds of years ago.

To the average person, Louisiana is not generally thought of as an important fur producing State; and yet, Louisiana furnishes approximately 75% of the entire muskrat catch of North America. Southern Louisiana is considered the greatest fur-producing area of the entire continent. Not only are muskrats plentiful, but also mink, otter and raccoon; and they provide an annual income of six to ten million dollars. What is even more surprising is the fact that this rich fur industry has only been realized during recent times—less than two generations.

The most interesting sections of North America today, from the standpoint of the trapper and the lover of virgin wilderness, is the Northwest. In western and northern Canada, and Alaska, there is an area almost half the size of the entire United States that is still to a large extent wilderness; and throughout this vast area are hundreds of men who spend the trapping season just about as they might have if they had trapped there a hundred years ago.

Trappers in the north are today of two principal types, just as they were in the early days of the Old West. There are independent trappers and company trappers. Some of these men only spend the open season on their extensive trap lines, and even travel and transport their supplies and furs by airplane. Some of them also act as guides on big-game hunting and fishing trips by sportsmen during the spring, summer and fall seasons. But when it comes to getting out and trapping fox or beaver or marten, they must know their stuff and they have but few modern advantages over their old-time counterparts. The animals are even smarter than they used to be; and forty below zero is just as cold.

The so-called company trapper is pretty much as he always

was. The Hudson's Bay Company today has many trading posts throughout Northern Canada and there is a similar local concern in practically every Alaskan frontier settlement. These places, as of old, still carry on extensive credit and debit accounting system with most of the local trappers. Throughout the summer the needs of the trappers and their families are supplied by the local "store"; and during the trapping season the indebtedness is repaid with the furs that are caught. If the trapper is ambitious and energetic, he generally does well. To be a successful trapper, no matter where the location may be, he must work diligently and know his business.

In many of the more remote sections the traders pay a flat price for skins. The price on each variety of fur is established at the beginning of the season and each skin brought in is credited for that amount. This practice, however, is not nearly as prevalent as it was in the earlier days. In most instances the trader is very fair.

Trapping grounds are considered just as much a piece of property as the rifle or food a man has in his cabin. This ownership is respected by the unwritten law of the wilds. Trapping grounds are inherited from father to son, and they can be sold or traded the same as any other possession. To encroach on another man's ground is considered the same as stealing, and many a shooting in the far north has resulted from such an offense. In spite of this priority of possession, however, there are plenty of open trapping grounds which can be had by adventurous newcomers who have the inclination and courage to enter this fascinating occupation.

The famous Alcan Highway, up to Alaska through western Canada, has made a vast area of good trapping grounds in the northwest more accessible than ever before; and it will see many a new pioneer heading north, with his auto packed with provisions, warm clothing and steel traps.

But, surprising as it may seem to many, it is not in the far north that the greatest number of fur-bearers are caught. Here are some government statistics for the 1945-46 trapping season on the comparative numbers of pelts taken: For fox, of all varieties: Alaska, 13,705; Iowa, 13,904; Illinois, 16,636; Minnesota, 23,218; Missouri, 26,563; Michigan, 52,017. For mink: Alaska, 31,339; Iowa, 48,145; Michigan, 53,400; Minnesota, 95,782; Louisiana, 168,598;

and for the grand total of all pelts of all varieties: Alaska, 223,173; Iowa, 624,565; Wisconsin, 1,291,758; Minnesota, 1,558,832; Louisiana, 8,869,609.

Whether you do your trapping amid the snow and ice of Alaska or the marshlands of Louisiana, however, the most important requirement for success is to have a thorough knowledge of the animal being sought. The trapper must be a naturalist, as well as an expert in the art of setting his trap.

The printed page can only be an elementary guide. Real knowledge of wild life is something which comes only from first hand experience. To some people, with a keen sense of observation, this comes quickly; but there are other folks who can wander through the woods or fields year after year and still miss the many little tell-tale things which seldom escape the naturalist-trapper.

One of the best ways to assure a successful winter trapping season, if circumstances permit, is to spend your summer holidays quietly observing the locations where you plan to set your traps. Train yourself to see and analyze all the little evidences which are left by the fur bearers. You'll be surprised how they can be pieced together and give you ideas for your winter program.

Never trap or kill fur bearers until the fur is prime. When you do this you only cheat yourself of top prices for the pelts.

CHAPTER IV

THE MUSKRAT

THE Muskrat (*Ondatra zibethica* and related forms) gets its
name from the musky odor produced by a pair of scent glands
about the size of lima beans, found on the males just under the skin
on their belly between the hind legs. The odor is penetrating,
although not considered unpleasant to most persons. The "rat"
part of this animal's name is derived from its slight resemblance
to the common variety of that name. As a matter of fact, the
muskrat is closely related to the Meadow Mouse (*Microtus penn-
sylvanicus* and related forms). In the early days of the fur trade
the muskrat was popularly known from coast to coast as "mus-
quash"—and "talking muskwash" became a common expression
in the north country to signify "talking fur business" or even
"just talking." In the Sioux Indian language the muskrat was
called *sinkpe* and the Osage Indians called him *taci*.

There are fourteen scientifically recognized varieties of muskrats in North America; and these constitute our most plentiful,
most widely distributed and most valuable of our present day fur
bearing animals. They are found from northern Alaska to the
Gulf of Mexico, and from Newfoundland and along our Atlantic
seaboard to the Pacific. The only places in the United States where
they do not exist is at the higher elevations of the Rocky Mountains and in some of the arid deserts of the Southwest. According

to official reports by government agencies of the United States and Canada, there were in the neighborhood of 18,000,000 musk-rats taken during the 1945-46 trapping season; and this figure does not take into account the unquestionably large number taken by farmer boys and others who did not report their catches to the authorities, nor those taken in many of the States where neither trappers or fur buyers are required to make such reports of furs taken. Only thirty-six of the forty-eight States require such reports.

Here are the recognized varieties of this valuable little fur-bearing animal, together with their range and distinguishing characteristics:

The Common Muskrat (*Ondatra zibethica zibethica*) is found in the east central and northeastern United States and southeastern Canada, from Nova Scotia and New Brunswick to western Minnesota, south as far as northern Georgia and Arkansas, but not along the Atlantic seaboard south of Delaware Bay. This variety has the largest distribution of any, covering almost all of the eastern half of the U.S., excepting the eastern half of Virginia, North and South Carolina; the southern half of Georgia, Alabama and Mississippi; and all of Florida and Louisiana. In coloration it is dark brown over the back with the head slightly darker, sides and underparts chestnut approaching whitish on belly and throat, blackish spot on chin and blackish around wrists and heels. An occasional black phase is found. Total length of the body averages between twenty-two and twenty-three inches, plus a ten-inch tail; and the weight runs about two pounds.

The Virginia Muskrat (*Ondatra zibethica macradon*) has a rather limited range along the Atlantic coast from Delaware Bay to Pamlico Sound and inland about as far as Raleigh, N.C. This is the largest of all the muskrats, generally running a good two inches longer than the common muskrat; but in color it is usually much lighter.

The Labrador Muskrat (*Ondatra zibethica aquilonia*) is found in Labrador and Ungava. It is very much like the common musk-rat except for its brighter and more richly colored fur.

The Newfoundland Muskrat (*Ondatra obscura*) is found only in Newfoundland. It is comparatively small in size, but par-

MUSKRAT

RIGHT HIND
AND RIGHT FORE
FOOT PRINTS

3"

TAIL DRAG

FLOATING LOG
SET

BAIT

UNDER WATER SETS

BAIT

SURFACE

LOG

TO
DEEP
WATER

WATER
LEVEL

BURROW
ENTRANCE

RUNWAY

ticularly dark in color—sometimes almost black. Another distinguishing feature is its large hind feet.

The Hudson's Bay Muskrat (*Ondatra zibethica alba*) ranges from the western shores of Hudson's Bay to eastern Saskatchewan and north to the Barren Grounds. This variety is somewhat larger than those in Newfoundland, but not as large as the common muskrat; and rather pale in color.

The Northwestern Muskrat (*Ondatra zibethica spatulata*) has its habitat over an area almost as large as that of the common muskrat, extending from western Saskatchewan across the northern three-quarters of Alberta and British Columbia, north to the Arctic Ocean and through that part of Alaska drained by the tributaries of the great Yukon River. This is another of the smaller varieties, but its color is a dark glossy brown, on the back, but fairly light sides and belly.

The Alaska Peninsula Muskrat (*Ondatra zibethica zalopha*) is found on the eastern part of the Alaska Peninsula and along the Pacific coast to Cook Inlet. It is about the same size as its nearest relative the Northwestern variety, although having a shorter tail, smaller hind feet; and the fur is somewhat lighter in color and lacking the silky gloss.

The Rocky Mountain Muskrat (*Ondatra zibethica osoyoosensis*) ranges from Puget Sound and southern British Columbia through most of Washington, Idaho and western Montana southward through the Rockies to northern New Mexico. This is one of the largest of the muskrats and is usually dark brown to blackish in color.

The Oregon Coast Muskrat (*Ondatra zibethica occipitalis*) is found on the coast of Oregon and in the northern Willametta Valley. It is about the size of the Rocky Mountain variety, but of a much paler and redder color.

The Nevada Muskrat (*Ondatra zibethica mergens*) is found in Nevada, western Utah, northeastern California, southeastern Oregon and the northern part of the Great Basin. It is not quite as large as the two previous varieties, and is pale in color, sometimes grayish brown.

The Arizona Muskrat (*Ondatra zibethica pallida*) ranges through Arizona, the Colorado River Valley and into Lower

California. This is the smallest of all the muskrats, and in color is a rusty red, with practically no long dark guard hairs on the back.

The Pecos Muskrat (*Ondatra zibethica ripensis*) has a very limited range through the Pecos Valley in Texas and New Mexico. It is almost as small as the Arizona variety, with an even shorter tail, but somewhat darker in color.

The Great Plains Muskrat (*Ondatra zibethica cinnamomina*) is found over a wide area through the great central plains region of the U.S. and into southern Canada. It is medium in size and pale or cinnamon brown in color.

The Louisiana Muskrat (*Ondatra rivalicia*) is found along the coast regions of Louisiana, inland to northern Calcasieu, Point Coupee and Tangipahoa parishes. This variety, of which so many millions have been caught, is one of the smaller muskrats. Its back is brownish black with but little of the reddish tinge found in other varieties, although the pelage is somewhat duller; and the underparts are much darker.

From the above it will be readily seen that the muskrat is found under practically every type of geographical condition existing in North America—semi-tropical marshes, Arctic tundra, plains, forest, mountains. They thrive in temperatures that reach 120°F. or hotter, as well as 60° below zero; and yet there is not a great deal of difference in their general appearance, habits or character of fur. Unlike many of our other fur bearers, they are native only to this continent, although attempts have been made to establish them in other parts of the world.

Although the distribution of the muskrat is fairly general throughout most parts of North America, there are some sections where they are much more plentiful than elsewhere. Their greatest abundance is unquestionably in the marshes extending inland from the Gulf Coast of Louisiana. During the 1945-46 season the official report for that State alone was 8,337,411. Another especially productive area is the marshes around Chesapeake Bay, where the largest, darkest and most valuable of all the muskrats are found. It has been unofficially estimated that about 2,000,000 of these fur bearers are taken annually along this Eastern Shore of Maryland. This latter figure has, however, been authoritatively disputed; and as the State of Maryland does not require either trappers or fur dealers to make annual reports on the number of furs taken or sold, no official records are available, although it is well known that the district is one of the most prolific for its area. A few of the other States which supply bona fide records give further evidence of muskrats distribution: Minnesota, 1,211,106; Ohio, 385,468; Iowa, 418,417; Alaska, 152,542; California, 56,425; Maine, 20,079. For comparison, the official figures for the season of 1940-41 for the same localities are given: Louisiana, 5,405,425; Minnesota, 867,-608; Ohio, 832,806; Iowa, 350,700; Alaska, 417,442; California, 68,318; Maine, 39,133. To go much further back, and as an indication that the muskrats have credibly survived a long and intensive period of trapping, a reliable source gives the catch for the season of 1864 as 2,850,000.

Before going into details as to how muskrats are trapped, it may be of interest to note some of the circumstances under which this remarkable crop of fur bearers is harvested in different parts of the continent.

In the State of Louisiana, the trapping of these animals was formerly a free-for-all proposition in which anyone could trap almost anywhere. Under these conditions many quarrels developed over the trapping on certain areas; and there were numerous shootings and some fatalities. But when the muskrat became more valuable, this method was changed. Now, practically all of this vast area of marsh land is either owned, leased, or controlled by individuals or corporations. Some corporations own many thousands of acres of these marsh lands. The actual trapping is done by the native population. The individual receives so much for each muskrat or mink or raccoon caught, skinned and dried. Naturally this amount varies with the market price of the fur. The trapper usually receives slightly less than one-half the value of the pelt.

These large marsh owners maintain a headquarters out on the marsh; cabins in which the trappers live; and a store stocked with food and necessary clothing. Many families move out and live in these cabins during the trapping season. The men do the actual trapping, and the women and children help in the skinning and drying. They also have cabins located at various places throughout the property, along the bayous or waterways. They maintain motor boats with which they visit these cabins two or three times a week, to deliver supplies and collect the fur.

Large areas in Georgia and most of Florida are occupied by the round tail rat. This animal lives about the same life as the muskrat, but it has no fur value.

On the Eastern Shore of Maryland, and around the Chesapeake Bay, conditions are somewhat different. Here, much of the marsh land is owned by farmers in connection with their farms. In some cases, city dwellers have purchased quite large areas of marsh land, upon which they have tenants who do a little farming of the tillable parts of the land, and care for the marsh and do the trapping on the share-the-profit plan. Here also it is usually less than one-half the value of the pelt which is received by the trapper.

The Canadian Government has worked out a system of control over the trapping industry, whereby it is possible for them to compile a very accurate report of the number of, and the average price received for, all the fur-bearing animals taken throughout the entire area each year.

Ten or twelve years ago, a citizen of Manitoba leased from the Canadian Government a large area of marsh land. He built some earth dams; dug some ditches; and did other work necessary to stabilize the water level on this area throughout the year. The result was that the annual production of muskrats more than doubled in two years.

The Government then decided that, rather than lease the Government-owned marsh lands to individuals, they would retain control and make the necessary improvements for the benefit of the native population. Since that time the water levels have been stabilized on large areas of formerly unproductive marshland, and the muskrat populations have increased to a remarkable extent.

Individual citizens or families are allotted certain areas, and are allowed to trap a stated number of muskrats. At the close of the season the skins are collected by Government employees, and each trapper is given credit for his skins. The fur is sold to the highest bidder. Thus everyone interested (the Government included) is receiving substantial returns from properties that were formerly unproductive.

The work being done by Ducks Unlimited, in cooperation with

the Canadian Government, to provide nesting and rearing grounds
for wild water fowl, is also creating ideal homes for muskrats;
and, given sufficient time, and with the present intelligent manage-
ment, the muskrat skins will pay the entire bill. The muskrat industry in Canada incidentally, is now in a very healthy and prosperous condition.

The economic importance of the muskrat comes from the fine
underfur which covers the skin beneath the longer, glistening
guard-hairs. The plucked or sheared pelts have a close resemblance
to similarly treated beaver or even fur seal, and a large part of
each year's catch is utilized in the manufacture of garments labeled
Hudson Seal or resembling genuine beaver.

Fortunately the muskrat is both a hardy and a prolific little
creature. In the marshlands of Maryland, where these animals have
been carefully studied by competent observers, females have been
known to have as many as five litters per year and the number of
young in a litter varying from three to twelve or even more—the
average is six or eight. This is probably also true of the Louisiana
marshes as well as other similar areas where the climate continues
moderate throughout the year. Under such extreme living conditions as are found in the mountainous regions and the northern
part of its range, however, it is doubtful if more than two litters
annually occur; although the muskrat does not hibernate and even
the coldest temperature has no undue effect upon its activity and
personal prosperity.

Marshes, ponds and stream banks are the natural home of the
muskrat. It is never found very far from water. In the marsh areas
they generally build winter houses of rushes and various water
plants, mixed with mud, although in summer their home may be
little more than nests in the tall grass. In some regions they burrow
into the stream banks, at the surface or below the water level,
with the underground nest above water at the end of the burrow.

They are expert swimmers, preferring to travel in the water
rather than on land. Still or slow-moving water is best suited to
their particular mode of life, although the mountain varieties
sometimes frequent even white-water. Along the sea coasts it is
not averse to brackish water, making its home in the salt marshes.
They are not particularly wary and can occasionally be seen in the

evening and early morning. And as their houses, trails through the grass and burrows plainly indicate their presence, it is quite easy for the trapper to find places to make his sets.

Their principal foods are the foliage, roots and bulbs of water plants, cat tails, sweet flag, three-cornered or three-square grass, wild rice, duck millet and reed grass. Willow shoots are sometimes cut by muskrats and stored as winter food. They are quite clean in their habits and in some sections of the country many persons consider them desirable as human food. They are even sold in some markets—called "swamp rabbits."

Their natural enemies are hawks, owls, mink, otters, weasels, foxes, wolves, and even pike and pickerel kill the young animals.

Each year the trapping of muskrats provides an enormous income for America's rural population. These little semi-aquatic animals are among the easiest of the fur bearers to trap; and although they have been trapped extensively for centuries, they are still found in large numbers where their natural environment has not been destroyed, and they have not learned to be wary of the trap.

If the trapping is to be done along a stream where the muskrats have burrowed into the bank, the first thing to do is determine the holes that are being used. This is not difficult, from their general appearance. The No. 1 Oneida Victor Trap or the No. 1 Oneida Jump Trap can be used successfully in places where there is plenty of water in which to drown the animals, because if they are not quickly drowned, they will surely twist or wring off their foot and escape in a crippled condition. With this in mind, the trap should be placed just inside the hole; be sure that it rests firmly and there is sufficient room for the rat to swim into it; and the chain should be drawn out its full length and staked to the bottom so that the captured muskrat will drown quickly.

Another good set is at the foot of the little paths or slides which muskrats use on leaving or entering the water. In such cases the trap should be set under about two inches of water, just where the trail enters the stream; and here also be sure to put the stake out in deeper water to insure quick drowning.

If the trapping is to be done in a marsh or around a pond, the traps can be set in the well-marked trails they make through the grass. Some trappers make their sets at the sides of the houses, although the game laws of certain states prohibit this, and many smart trappers refrain from this practice. Too much disturbance around a house may cause the inhabitants to move to another locality. If your State game laws permit, and you decide to set traps beside a muskrat house, be sure that the location permits staking the trap in sufficiently deep water for quick drowning. The commotion and alarm caused by a trapped muskrat thrashing about on the side of a house, or a wring-off crawling back into the home den, is apt to prove disastrous to future trapping.

The greatest problem in amateur trapping has been the wring-offs. If a muskrat is not quickly drowned, it is pretty sure to twist off its foot and escape. Careful investigations have proven that a great number of these crippled animals die in their houses or dens, and are a total loss to all concerned. Under circumstances where it is impossible to insure the quick drowning of the caught muskrats, the following traps should be used: No. 1 Victor "Stop Loss," No. 1 Oneida Jump "Stop Loss" or the Two Trigger Trap. These traps have been specially developed to prevent wring-offs where trapping is done under such conditions; and thousands of muskrat trappers will testify to their efficiency.

Trapping is more a matter of keen observation and ingenuity on the part of the trapper, than following out any specific instructions. For example, you may find a place in shallow sluggish water where bits of freshly cut water plants or water grass and other indications that muskrats have fed there. By careful observation you may determine that this is one of the places where the animals regularly come to feed. Here then is another place to make a set. It may be best to place the trap or traps under-water right in the midst of the "feed"; or there may be a trail or narrow approach where the set should be made. But in any event either place the trap so the muskrat will be drowned or use a stop-loss or two-trigger type of trap.

One of the most easily recognized signs on a muskrat stream are the places where these animals haul out to eat or just to sun themselves. This may be an old log, a small snag, stump or rock. If these places are being used you will find "droppings" on them. If these are brown and dry, they are old; if grey and moist, the muskrat have recently been using the place. If it is an old log that runs down under water, make your set on it under about two inches of water. If it is a rock, you can probably figure out where they generally make a landing—and do the same there. A little grass or a few water soaked leaves may help to conceal the trap, although this is not always necessary. If there are no such hauling-out places on your trapping stream or pond, give some thought to placing an old log or two there for their use. This should be done in the summer or at least a considerable time before you start trapping, so they will become accustomed to using it before you start setting traps. Incidentally, the baiting of sets such as these often pays—parsnips, apples, carrots, or sweet flag roots can be used.

Trapping in the cold climates, however, presents considerably more of a problem. As all furs are prime only in mid-winter, this means a rather rugged experience for trappers in the north country and other sections where Ol' Man Winter rules with a despotic determination. But to those who know the big north woods or even its bleak open wastes, when the streams are frozen and the ground is covered with snow, there is no more fascinating time of year. Just to be able to read all the stories written in the freshly fallen snow, to anyone who understands their language, is well worth all the other more or less unpleasant inconveniences. Trapping under low temperature conditions is much more difficult and takes considerably more ingenuity. Traps freeze, become deeply covered with new snow and your own tracks tell even more to the wary fur bearers than their tracks mean to you. But fortunately for the muskrat trapper and his luck, that little creature is about the least wary of all the fur-bearing animals.

Muskrats do not hibernate even in the coldest parts of their range and are active under the ice, regularly going back and forth between their houses or dens and the feeding grounds. But under these conditions they are much more susceptible to baiting. The best method of trapping, however, must be largely governed by actual conditions—whether the ice is thick or thin; the water deep or shallow, swift or still; depth of snow; the temperature around freezing or many degrees below zero. Here is where the trapper's ingenuity is really put to the test. For every condition there must be a plan that will prove effective.

Although muskrats can, if necessary, spend their time under ice, they do like to get out on the surface, if only to sit near an air hole. Find these, for they are easy places to make good catches. If the water is shallow, and the temperature is not so low that the trap will freeze solid during the night, set your trap under water, even if you have to rake up the bottom to make a platform so that the trap will be sufficiently close to the surface. If the water is deep, you can insert a log or a plank in the air hole, with the trap attached firmly to it just below the surface of the water (see diagram, page 25). You can even cover the air hole with a canopy of dry grass etc., to help keep it from freezing over.

In making all deep under-water sets, it should be kept in mind that light pan action is necessary. When swimming, a muskrat does not step on the pan of a trap with anything of the force that it does when walking on the dry ground or coming out of the water. Set the pan lightly, so that it will spring the trap at the slightest touch. Deep water sets are, of course unaffected by freezing.

The cold weather muskrat trapper will find that using certain special equipment will make his work a great deal more comfortable as well as profitable. A shoulder length rubber or waterproof "glove" is almost a must. With this you can reach down into the water to search for the right spot to set the traps etc., etc., and keep comparatively warm and dry. Some sort of an ice chisel—welded onto about a three foot piece of tubular steel for lightness—will pay well; as well as a light axe with a hammer and nails, wire, etc. But the most valuable of all the things you will take on this trap line will be your own keen powers of observation and ingenuity.

The importance of fur as a source of farm income is often overlooked. This is particularly true of the muskrat. Yet with only a little effort and very slight expenditure, money can pleasantly be earned. The animals are trapped in winter when farm work as well as income is normally low. Throughout America, trap lines are helping farmers meet expenses, purchase better equipment and educate their children. It has always poured a steady stream of cash into the pockets of ambitious and enterprising American farm boys.

Like other farm crops, fur yields most when cultivated. This also applies to muskrats, and is more practical than it sounds.

The first step toward cultivation is to stop thinking of your swampland and marshy places as worthless spots, to be drained or used as dumping grounds. Consider them as acreage that can be made profitable. Conserve the cover and food supply, by fencing against pasturing stock. Prevent grazing along stream banks. Here grow the water plants and willow shoots that are the staple food for the prolific and profitable muskrats. If necessary, build small dams to maintain a constant water level. Provide homes for them and their fur will repay you many times over.

Muskrats are the backbone of the fur industry. Get your share.

Muskrats should always be skinned "cased" with the pelt side out. Commercially made adjustable drying frames of heavy spring-wire are the most practical means of drying the skins.

CHAPTER V

THE BEAVER

THE Beaver (*Castor canadensis* and related forms) is the king of fur-bearing animals. The skin of this animal was the basis of the early fur trade, which was responsible for the exploration and early development of a large part of North America. All other furs were, for nearly two hundred years, secondary in importance; and throughout most of that time the beaver skin was a standard of valuation in barter and exchange, much as the American dollar is today. Industries were developed and depended upon it; and many great fortunes were founded upon it.

The beaver was very plentiful throughout most of North America when the white man first began settling along the Atlantic seaboard of this continent. The Indians killed beaver for food and used their skins for clothing; but they attached no particular trade value to them. But the beaver and its valuable skin were already known to these first settlers in America, for the animal was also native to Europe and Asia, where its place in trade had been well established.

In 1733, near Hudson's Bay, for a full-grown beaver skin one could buy half a pound of beads, or one pound of Brazil tobacco, or a half-pound of thread. A gallon of brandy cost four beaver skins; broadcloth, two beaver skins a yard; blankets, six beaver skins each; powder, one beaver skin for a pound and a half; shot, one beaver skin for five pounds; and so on through a long list. And the comparative values of other furs was: one beaver was equaled by three martens, one fox, one moose, two deer, one wolf or ten pounds of feathers.

A hundred years later, or about 1833, we find a blanket worth ten beaver skins; a gun, twenty; eighteen bullets, one skin. The gun cost 22 shillings ($5.50), and the twenty beaver skins were worth in London £ 32 10s. ($162.50). A gill of powder, costing one and a half pence, or a knife costing fourpence, or a dozen brass buttons were exchanged for one beaver skin.

But the beaver skin, so long the staple of the fur trade, received its death blow by the invention of the silk hat. Up to about 1842 the principal use of beaver skins had been for the making of felt for the manufacture of "beaver" hats, which had been very popular. As early as 1638, Charles I of England had issued a proclamation prohibiting the use of any material except "pure beaver wool" in the manufacture of such hats. The introduction of the silk hat, however, literally caused the bottom completely to drop out of the beaver skin market. In 1839 the price on the London Market had risen to 27s.6d. (about $6.87 in present day currency); but by 1846 the price had dropped to 3s.5d. (about 85 cents)—all due to the silk hat! So far as the beaver was concerned, however, this was an exceedingly fortunate turn of events; for it is quite probable that these animals might have been entirely exterminated if their intensive trapping had been continued.

Beaver are today far from as plentiful as they once were. They are still distributed pretty generally throughout the length and breadth of North America, although their ranges are restricted to comparatively small areas in many of the wilder sections from Alaska and Labrador to the Rio Grande. There are today fourteen scientifically recognized varieties:

The Canadian Beaver (*Castor canadensis canadensis*) is found across practically all of Canada and Alaska nearly as far north as the continent extends, and as far south into the United States as North Carolina, Tennessee, Missouri, Kansas, Colorado, Idaho and Oregon. In size this variety runs about 43 inches in length, with a tail about 16 inches long and 4½ inches broad; the weight ranging from 30 to about 68 pounds, occasionally considerably heavier.

In color the upper parts are a rich dark brown, with long chestnut brown guard hairs and the soft short underfur without any reddish tinge; the underparts are somewhat lighter in tone. There is but little difference in the sexes, either in size or color.

The Cook Inlet Beaver (*Castor canadensis belugae*) is found in the Cook Inlet region of Alaska, south to Stuart Lake, British Columbia. This variety is somewhat larger than the Canadian beaver, with the upperparts cinnamon to tawny in color.

The Admiralty Beaver (*Castor canadensis phaeus*) is found only on Admiralty Island, Alaska. The upperparts are dark seal-brown, with the long guard hairs and the ears almost black. It is smaller in the body, although the tail is longer than the Canadian.

The Vancouver Island Beaver (*Castor canadensis leucodonta*) is found only on Vancouver Island, British Columbia. The upperparts are cinnamon-buff and the general coloration paler than the preceding. In size, however, it is generally larger.

The Pacific Beaver (*Castor canadensis pacificus*) ranges along the Pacific slope mainland from southern Oregon to Alaska. The upperparts are dark, glossy chestnut, with the underparts seal brown. This variety also is larger than the Canadian.

The Sonora or Broad-tailed Beaver (*Castor canadensis frondator*) is found in the southwestern states from Wyoming and Montana to Mexico. Its upperparts are a russet color, with the sides wood-brown. It has a particularly broad tail and is generally somewhat larger than Canadian.

The Rio Grande Beaver (*Castor canadensis mexicanus*) is found on the Rio Grande drainage regions of Texas and New Mexico. This is a comparatively small beaver with pale dull chestnut coloration. It is palest on the cheeks and rump.

The Texas Beaver (*Castor canadensis texensis*) is found in a limited region drained by the Rio Colorado, in eastern Texas. It is a large and pale variety, greatly resembling the Sonora beaver.

The Shasta Beaver (*Castor subauratus shastensis*) is now apparently extinct, but formerly was found in Shasta County, California, or the eastern slope of the Sierra Nevada mountains. (No accurate description of its size or coloration are available.)

The Golden Beaver (*Castor subauratus subauratus*) is found only on the drainage of the Tuolumme and San Joaquin Rivers in

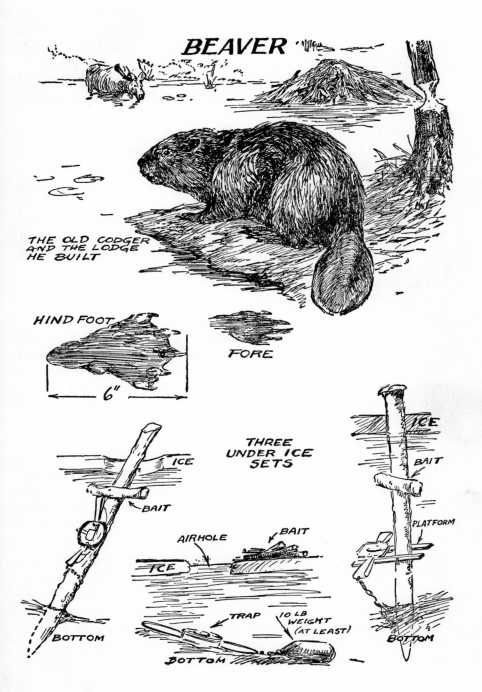

BEAVER

THE OLD CODGER
AND THE LODGE
HE BUILT

HIND FOOT

FORE

6"

THREE
UNDER ICE
SETS

ICE

BAIT

BOTTOM

AIRHOLE

BAIT

ICE

TRAP

10 LB
WEIGHT
(AT LEAST)

BOTTOM

ICE

BAIT

PLATFORM

BOTTOM

California. It is a large beaver with upperparts dark hazel to clay color and underparts sepia.

The Woods Beaver (*Castor canadensis michiganensis*) is found in the Upper Peninsula region of Michigan. It is large in size and its color very dark, with the ears and feet black.

The Missouri River Beaver (*Castor canadensis missouriensis*) ranges through the drainage of the Missouri River from Montana south and east to Nebraska. This is one of the smallest varieties, with upperparts bright hazel brown and the underparts smoky gray.

The Carolina Beaver (*Castor canadensis carolinensis*) is found in North Carolina southward to northern Florida and the Gulf of Mexico, west to eastern Texas. This is one of the larger varieties, with a broader tail; and is bright hazel in coloration.

The Newfoundland Beaver (*Castor caecator*) is found only in Newfoundland and may be extinct today. (No description available.)

An idea of the present numbers of beaver found in North America can probably best be indicated by giving a few statistics regarding the most recent catches as reported by official governmental agencies. In the United States eighteen States and Alaska reported a total of 88,563 beaver reported for 1945-46; as against a total of 78,468 for the same sections for the season of 1939-40. In the most recent report Montana led with 16,468; then Michigan, 15,296; Alaska, 9,553; Minnesota, 9,477; and on down to Texas with only 137. Nearly all of the States showed a noticeable increase over the 1939-40 season, except Alaska with 31,397 for the earlier period. In Canada the latest official report indicates a total of 130,779 beaver taken in all provinces, as compared to 90,-123 for the 1940-41 trapping season. This makes a total of 219,-342 beaver taken in North America for 1945-46. And when we consider that the estimate for the year 1864 was only 130,000, it would indicate that the trapping business in this particular fur bearer is definitely better today than it has been in the past.

Pennsylvania was without wild beaver for a period of at least seventy years prior to 1917. Early in the Spring of 1917 the conservation authorities of the State of Wisconsin presented one pair of beaver to Dr. Joseph Kalfbus, then Executive Secretary of the

Pennsylvania Game Commission. These beaver were liberated in Cowley Run in Cameron County, Pennsylvania. They at once went to work, built a dam and house, and the following summer raised a family of young. The Pennsylvania Board of Game Commissioners, after keeping this pair and their offspring under observation for some time, decided that it was entirely possible and desirable to reestablish the beaver in Pennsylvania.

During the winter of 1919 arrangements were made with the Canadian Government, and twenty-five pair of beaver were purchased for delivery in the spring of 1920. These beaver were liberated in game refuges in the northern or mountainous part of the State. They thrived and multiplied to such an extent that in 1934, after twelve years of protection, the first open trapping season was declared from March 1st to April 10, 1934. During that period, 6,521 fine prime beaver were trapped, pelted and sold by the native trappers of Pennsylvania.

The beaver is not only a valuable fur bearer, but a mighty fascinating creature. Space does not here permit telling but a small part of the story of the beaver. Their very industrious community life has long been the subject of interest and admiration among both scientists and trappers. The following account was written by the noted naturalist, Thomas Pennant in 1785; and while it is somewhat glamorized in the colorful language of the period, it is sufficiently accurate, basically, to bear repeating:

"These (the beaver) are the most sagacious and industrious of animals. They live in society and unite in their labors, for the good of the commonwealth they form. They erect edifices, superior in contrivance to the human beings. In order to form a habitation, they select a level piece of ground, with a small rivulet running in the vicinity. To effect their works, a community of two to three hundred assemble: every individual bears his share in the laborious preparation. Some fall trees of great size, by gnawing them asunder with their teeth, in order to form beams or piles; others are employed in rolling the pieces to the water; others dive, and scrape holes with their feet in order to fix them; and another set exert their efforts to rear them in their proper places. A fifth party is busied in collecting twigs to wattel the piles; a sixth in collecting earth, stones and clay; others carry it on their broad tails to the proper places and with their feet beat and temper the earth into mortar, or ram it between the piles, or plaster the inside of the houses."

Slightly exaggerated and with some discrepancies, nevertheless, the foregoing does give an excellent picture of the busy activity of a colony of beavers, and no one can deny them credit for being the most industrious and about the most clever of all the fur-bearing animals.

Beaver are strictly vegetarians. In summer they feed on aquatic plants, grass, roots, and the twigs and bark of aspen, cottonwood and willow trees. In winter it is merely the twigs and bark of trees. You will never find them very far from a waterway or lake in the vicinity of a good stand of aspen, poplar, cottonwood or willow. It makes no difference how large the trees may be, and although they are unable to climb to reach the twigs and bark, they can always cut down the trees to get them. As soon as a tree is felled, the branches are cut off and dragged to the nearest water-course from where they are towed to the family house or under-water burrow in the bank, to be stripped and enjoyed at leisure. Plenty of these branches are also put away for winter use—being fastened to the bottom of the stream or lake, where they can be gotten even when ice completely covers the water.

The expression "busy as a beaver" is a true reference to these animals. In places where they are not disturbed, beaver may be active during the twenty-four hours of the day; although sunset to sunrise is their real working time. They are the most skillful engineers of the animal kingdom.

Much misinformation is attributed to the beaver's large hairless, scaly, flat, paddle-shaped tail. Despite popular belief it is not used as a sled on which to transport the materials used in their building operations; or as a platter on which to eat its meals. It is, however, used as a rudder while swimming and as a signal gun to slap on the surface of the water to warn the rest of the colony of the approach of danger; and to maintain the individual's balance when standing erect.

These animals are apparently monogamous, with but one per-manent mate; the young are born in late March to May, de-pending largely on the latitude; there are from two to six in a litter; and the young generally stay with the parents at least a full year.

Beaver pelts are never at their best until about February 1st. They are classed as fall, winter and spring pelts. Beaver taken in the spring months are worth at least 25% more than fall-caught pelts. In any well regulated beaver trapping operation they should be taken only during the months of February, March, or early April as after this time they commence to show signs of shedding.

In using the steel trap for beaver, nothing smaller than a No. 3 trap should be used. As it is absolutely necessary to drown the animal at once, a weight, either a stone or casting of at least ten pounds, should be securely wired to the trap. A wire should be attached to the trap chain of sufficient length to allow the beaver to plunge into water deep enough to drown it. Traps should never be set, staked or fastened away from water or in shallow water, as a beaver struggles frantically to escape and will either break or bite his leg off above the trap. Also, the disturbance he makes will cause all other beaver in the same pond to be trap-shy.

This drowning process can be modified in several ways, such as the sliding pole or a large stone with wire attached thrown into deep water; but experienced beaver trappers are agreed that the ten or twelve pound weight securely fastened directly to the trap is far the best method.

In placing the trap to catch a beaver it must be remembered this animal does not use the front feet while swimming, but holds them at rest at its sides. The first part of a beaver to strike the shore line is its throat or breast. The trap should be placed back from the water or in water shallow enough so the animal is in a walking position before reaching the trap.

Beaver can be induced to come ashore at desirable places by placing a fresh aspen limb with the tips at the water's edge, and tying it fast so it cannot be dragged into the water. Thus, they can get a taste of it but must come out over the trap to get more. This is a good set for early springtime. After living all winter on the water-logged food they have stored under the ice, they are eager for fresh aspen and will take it readily. The temptation will be great at times to set traps in the paths or shallow water where they travel from place to place, but if there is not water deep enough to drown the beaver, the trapped animal may not be there in the morning.

It is also an unwise policy to set traps beside a beaver house. You may find the family has suddenly moved away.

Most of the beaver that are taken in the northern States, Canada and Alaska, are caught through the ice. The methods are very similar to those used in catching muskrats, although the beaver is of course a much larger and stronger animal, as well as being considerably more wary and more difficult to trap. There are a number of good methods for taking these fur bearers—but here again the trapper must use his own good judgment and adopt the ways and means which best fit the particular circumstances of his own trapping grounds.

If you have the opportunity, time will be well spent in familiarizing yourself with your beaver trapping grounds in the fall before the ice forms. Find out where the beaver are making their food cache, in relation to the house or bank burrow in which they are living. With this information you will know the route they will regularly travel after the ice forms.

Nothing less than a No. 3 trap should be used for beaver—either the jump trap or double spring variety—and some prefer the No. 4 or No. 14 Oneida Jump. The jump trap will be found somewhat easier to make most of the popular sets. The beaver trapper also uses a considerable amount of strong soft wire; and his equipment should include a good pair of pliers with wire snipping attachment, a good small axe, nails, and for comfort, a waterproof glove with gauntlet that reaches well to the shoulder.

When you go to the trapping grounds to set out your first traps, select a dead dry pole long enough to reach from above the ice to well into the mud bottom at an angle of about 45°. Cut a notch in the pole at a point that will be about half way between the ice and the bottom, in such a manner that the trap will set about level when the pole is in position. These poles can be prepared before winter sets in. Now wire the trap firmly in the notch, so it will stay in set position but can be pulled loose by the beaver when caught. Staple the chain securely to the pole below the trap. Also fasten a green fresh pole, about one and a half or two inches in diameter, of aspen or gray birch, to the pole above where the trap is set. This "bait" should be long enough to reach from about two inches above the trap to the surface of the ice. When the set is ready to be made, cut a hole in the ice at a suitable spot between the beaver's house or bank den and their food cache and push the lower end of your pole securely into the bottom so that it will stand at the 45° angle with the bait and trap facing the house or den—and your set is complete. This type works best where the water is three or four feet deep, although it can be used in much deeper water. If the ice is thick, it may be well to cover the hole with long grass or brush, to kill the bright glow of light which the hole otherwise admits.

In places where the water is only a foot and a half or so deep, this set can be modified by driving a dead dry pole straight down into the bottom and wiring several green bait sticks to it and setting one or more traps directly on the bottom. But be sure and have the trap securely fastened to the dead pole and the latter imbedded securely in the bottom, or you may lose the whole outfit.

Where beaver build their dams on mountain streams, the water seldom freezes over entirely where the water enters the pond, or where it flows over the dam. The beaver also generally keep air holes open near the shore where the water is shallow. At any such places you can secure fresh aspen or gray birch tops for bait, just beyond the opening. The traps should be set on the bottom under the edge of the ice—using a wire long enough to allow the animal to plunge back under the ice and drown.

The broken dam set is effective whether or not there is ice on the pond. Cut a hole three or four inches deep and a foot or so wide in the dam so that the water will spill through. Even in quite low temperature this will keep running, if it is below the surface of the ice. Cut the hole at a place where the bottom of the pond is about eight or ten inches below the hole and set your trap there. The beaver will not lose much time in undertaking to repair the hole in their dam. The hole should not be too close to the trap, because it is apt to be sprung by the sticks and other material that is brought to make the repair; but when the beaver stand on their hind feet while pushing the material into place, they will put a hind foot in the trap.

In all cases it is well to stain new traps, to remove their bright appearance and make them appear more like the brown bottom of the pond. This can be done by boiling the traps in a strong solution of maple bark or alder for an hour or so and leaving them in the solution for a week or so.

There are other methods of setting traps for beaver; but the trapper who learns to analyze the situations as he finds them and by his own ingenuity develop modifications of the above suggestions, is sure of success.

The proper skinning and handling of the pelts after they are taken is almost as important as the trapping. Here is the correct way to skin one of these fur bearers:

Cut around both fore and hind feet just below the fur or cut the hind feet off. Cut skin loose around the legs as far as possible from outside.

Cut around tail just clear of fur.

Make straight cut from center of lower jaw down center of belly through vent to connect with cut made around tail.

Commence at lower jaw, skin back both ways, being careful not to cut or score the hide.

Loosen skin well down the side of neck and over ribs.

By loosening skin on legs, they will pull out through the holes made when cut was made around feet.

Do not slit the skin on any of the legs.

After all legs are pulled out, skin well down both sides, turn carcass over and loosen skin around base of tail.

The skin cannot be pulled from a beaver—it must be cut loose all the way, therefore, beginners should use great care and plenty of time as every cut reduces the value of the pelt. By using great care and working slowly, the skin can be removed practically clean of flesh or fat. This is desirable as the flesh and fat is difficult to remove after the skin is dry.

If you nail the skin to a board surface, be sure to tack up strips or make some provision so the air can get to the fur side or the fur may mold and spoil. The nails should be placed quite close together—about three-fourths of an inch to an inch apart. Start at the head and tail, but don't pull too tightly. When completely nailed, the width should be approximately the same as the length.

CHAPTER VI

THE SKUNK

SOME one once said: "If all things were equal, the skunk would be the King of Beasts!"—and this was not meant as a compliment. That little matter of intensive odor, with which these animals have become so proficient, has caused their name to become an opprobrious epithet. But the skunk is far more infamous among those who know little or nothing about him, than among those who have trapped him extensively and know him intimately. As a matter of fact he is normally a comparatively clean creature; when properly de-scented makes a nice pet; has flesh that is edible; and, to many who have had much experience, does not have a particularly offensive odor. As far as the odor is concerned, however, it is like sugar in coffee—too much is far more than enough! And there are many who will intensely dispute all the nice things which may be said about the skunk.

While we are on the subject of this most distinguishing characteristic of the skunks, it may prove interesting to go into a little serious information on the matter. The fluid in question is secreted in glands about three quarters of an inch in diameter, on each side of the rectum. Similar glands exist in other animals such as the wolverine, weasel, badger, mink etc., although in the skunks they reach the maximum of development, and their secretion acquires qualities which makes it the most penetrating, diffusible and intolerable of all the animals. Each gland is a sort of sac, enveloped with muscles and equipped with a duct to convey the secretion to an outlet on each side of the anus. Forcible erection of the tail is accompanied by a sharp compression of the muscles which envelop the sacs, and the liquid is squirted out just like squeezing the bulb of a syringe. The secretion is entirely under the voluntary control of the animal. It is purely a means of self-defense, although there is reason to suppose that the evacuation must recur at intervals simply to avoid over-distention of the continually secreting organ with its own product. The fluid is limited in quantity, and, having been discharged, the animal is harmless until the sacs are again filled by gradual secretion. They can, however, make more than one discharge. Ordinarily, the skunk is no more odorous than most other animals. The sacs can be deactivated by a veterinarian by a surgical operation; and when thus operated on, when the animals are young, they make quite desirable pets.

Under a microscope, the fluid has the appearance of molten gold, or like quicksilver of the finest golden color, made up of minute globules. To the eye, it is a pale bright or glistening yellow, with specks floating in it. That this fluid is dangerous to the eyesight of other animals, dogs and human beings is well established, and permanent blindness can result if a sufficient amount of it gets directly into the eyes. But to try to say something nice about this obnoxious fluid, there is an old belief that the odor is a good cure for asthma.

The story is told by Audubon, the great naturalist, of an asthmatic clergyman who procured the glands of a skunk, which he kept tightly corked in a smelling bottle, to be applied to his nose when his symptoms appeared. He believed he had discovered a cure for his distressing malady, and rejoiced thereat; but on one occasion he uncorked his bottle in the pulpit, and drove his congregation out of the church.

The matter of contracting hydrophobia from skunk bite is also worthy of comment. It is well known that skunks may contract hydrophobia when bitten by a "mad" coyote; and under such circumstances it is possible for a human being to contract the malady if bitten by the infected skunk. There are authentic records of death as a result. Such occurrences are rare, however, and the

SKUNKS

HOGNOSED SKUNK

LITTLE SPOTTED SKUNK

COMMON SKUNK

FORE

2½"

HIND

RUNNING TRACKS

CUBBY SET

FLAT STONE

BAIT

STAKES

ROCK PILE SET

BAIT

BURIED TRAP

average skunk is no more dangerous in this respect than other wild animals. It is the little spotted skunk which particularly has the reputation for giving hydrophobia when it bites a human being; and as a result of this it is sometimes called the "Hydrophobia Skunk" in certain sections of the Southwest. There seems to be a difference, however, between the hydrophobia contracted from skunk-bite (*rabies mephitica*) and that resulting from dog-bite (*rabies canina*), although in both instances a period ranging from ten days to several months may elapse between the time of being bitten and serious developments.

There are two general types of skunks—the large Striped Skunk and the much smaller Spotted Skunk. In all there are thirty-two scientifically recognized varieties in North America, of which fourteen are the Striped Skunk or Common Skunk (*Mephitis mephitis* and related forms); one variety of the Northern Hooded Skunk (*Mephitis macroura milleri*); four varieties of the Hog-nosed or White-backed Skunk (*Conepatus mesoleucus mearnsi* and related forms) and thirteen varieties of the Little Spotted Skunk or Polecat (*Spilogale putorius* and related forms). They all have a great deal in common, although there is considerable variation in many of their habits. In one form or another they are found throughout the United States and well up into Canada, ranging considerably farther north in the West than in the East.

Although the list is a long one it is given completely though briefly, as local trappers may find it interesting to determine the particular classification of skunk which inhabits their own district.

The Canada Skunk (*Mephitis mephitis*) is found throughout the most of eastern Canada, from Nova Scotia, through Quebec and northern Ontario. It has a broad white band from the top of its head to the shoulders and continuing in two broad white stripes to the base of the tail. Generally there is a small white stripe along the top of its nose joining the broader stripe. The rest of the body is glistening black, except the tail which may be black and white in varying proportions, with all the long tail hairs white at the base. The sexes are colored alike, although the female is generally a little smaller in size. The body of the male generally runs about twenty-four to twenty-five inches in length, with the tail verte-brae about seven to eight inches. The average weight is about eight pounds. The length of the female is usually about one and a half to two inches shorter.

The Eastern Skunk (*Mephitis nigra*) ranges through the New England and Middle Atlantic States as far west as Indiana and south to Virginia. The white stripes are usually broader than the Canada variety; and the tail is longer and the hairs tipped with white. It is slightly smaller in size than the Canada variety.

The Northern Plains Skunk (*Mephitis hudsonica*) ranges through Western Canada from Manitoba to British Columbia east of the Cascades, south into Colorado, Nebraska and Minnesota. This variety is quite similar in coloration to the Canada skunk except that the tail is heavier and bushier and the animal is quite a bit larger.

The Florida Skunk (*Mephitis elongata*) ranges through most of Florida, north into North Carolina and West Virginia and west along the Gulf Coast to the Mississippi River. It is distinguished by its particularly long tail, which is marked with white on the sides and a long white tip, and the white stripes along the back are generally very broad. It is medium in size, as compared to Canada.

The Louisiana Skunk (*Mephitis mesomelas mesomelas*) is found along the western side of the Mississippi Valley from northern Louisiana northward into Missouri; westward along the Gulf Coast to Matagorda Bay; and up the Red River Valley to Wichita Falls. This variety is comparatively small in size; with short tail, usually entirely black; and the white stripes sometimes do not reach to the base of the tail.

The Long-tailed Texas Skunk (*Mephitis mesomelas varians*) ranges through southern and western Texas and eastern New Mexico, northward into Oklahoma, Colorado, Kansas and Nebraska. In color it is typical, but has a tail more than twice as long as that of the Canada skunk.

The Illinois Skunk (*Mephitis mesomelas avia*) is found in the prairie regions of Illinois, eastern Iowa and western Indiana. It resembles the Canada skunk except in certain skull characteristics which mean little to the trapper.

The Arizona Skunk (*Mephitis estor*) is found in Arizona, western New Mexico and southward into Mexico. It has an unusual amount of white on the body, with white on the upper part of tail nearly concealing the black.

The California Skunk (*Mephitis occidentalis occidentalis*) is found in northern and central California, northward into the Willamette Valley, Oregon. The white stripes are of medium width and tail long. It is large in size.

The Southern California Skunk (*Mephitis occidentalis holzneri*) ranges through southern California. It is similar to the California skunk, except that it averages about six inches shorter in size.

The Puget Sound Skunk (*Mephitis occidentalis spissigrada*) ranges along the coast regions of Puget Sound, Washington and northern Oregon. It has more than ordinary white, with the stripes dividing about the middle of the back and much white on the tail.

The Great Basin Skunk (*Mephitis occidentalis major*) is found in eastern Oregon, northern California and Nevada, east to the Wasatch Mountains in Utah. This is one of the largest of the skunks, with broad white stripes dividing about middle of the back and with a large black tail.

The Cascade Skunk (*Mephitis occidentalis notata*) ranges through southern Washington and northern Oregon, east to the Cascades. This variety has narrower white stripes which do not connect at the rear part of the body. The tail is black with little or no white.

The Broad-nosed Skunk (*Mephitis platyrhina*) is found only in Kern County, California. The white stripes are medium in breadth; and the tail has an indistinct white stripe on the back. This is one of the largest of the skunks.

The Northern Hooded Skunk (*Mephitis macroura milleri*) is found in southern Arizona south into Mexico. There are two phases of this variety; one in which the upperpart of the body is nearly all white and the underparts black; while in the other phase the upperpart is black, with narrow white stripes on the sides and white on the underside of the tail. Variations of both phases are found. It is medium in size.

The hog-nosed skunks are about the same size and build as the varieties previously described, although they have a single broad white band extending unbroken from the crown of the head to the end of the tail. Another difference, and the one which gives them their name, is that the nose is entirely naked or hog-like. They also have a much smaller and less bushy tail. The white band down the back sometimes has a yellowish tinge and spreads out to cover most of the rear part of the back. The rest of the body, is, of course, black; but this generally has a rather brownish tinge, rather than the rich glistening black of the Canada skunk and its related forms.

The Mearns Hog-nosed Skunk (*Conepatus mesoleucus mearnsi*) is found in western Texas, east as far as Austin and south into Mexico. This is the type variety as above described.

The Swamp Hog-nosed Skunk or White-backed Skunk (*Conepatus mesoleucus telmalestes*) inhabits a limited area in Texas in the counties of Liberty, Hardin, San Jacinto, Montgomery and Harris. The whole upperpart of the body, from the eyes to the end of the tail, are white; the rest of the body black. It is comparatively small in size.

The Arizona Hog-nosed Skunk (*Conepatus mesoleucus venaticus*) is found in southeastern Arizona and the nearby region of New Mexico. It is similar to the Mearns variety, except in certain cranial characteristics.

The Texas Hog-nosed Skunk (*Conepatus leuconotus texensis*) ranges along a limited area of the Gulf Coast of Texas from Arkansas County to the mouth of the Rio Grande. This is about the largest of all the skunks, although the white on the back is much narrower and sometimes the rump is entirely black; with the underside of the tail more black.

The Spotted Skunk or Polecat is much smaller and less robust than its close relatives previously described. It is about the size of a half-grown house-cat and more weasel-like in general build. In color it too is a pattern of black and white, although the white markings on the upperparts consist of four rather broken white stripes running parallel from the neck backward to about the middle of the body; another white stripe extends from behind each foreleg back to the rump, where it curves up onto the back, crossing at right angles to the posterior ends of back-stripes; and still another, more broken white stripe, extends upward across each rump. There are also white spots or blotches on the forehead between the eyes, on the side of each rump and on each side of the tail at the base. They are found throughout most of the United States.

The Alleghenian Spotted Skunk (*Spilogale putorius*) is found in Mississippi, Alabama, western Georgia and South Carolina, and along the Alleghenies to northern Virginia. It is the "type" variety as above described.

The Florida Spotted Skunk (*Spilogale ambarvalis*) is found in the southern half of the eastern part of Florida. It is smaller than the above, with shorter tail and more white.

The Prairie Spotted Skunk (*Spilogale interrupta*) is found in southern Minnesota, Iowa, Nebraska, Kansas, Missouri, Oklahoma and south into eastern Texas to about the middle of the State. It is blacker than the type variety; without white tip on the tail; and stripes narrow and more interrupted.

The Gulf Spotted Skunk (*Spilogale indianola*) ranges through the coastal region of Texas and Louisiana. In coloration it resembles the Prairie variety, except that the tail has a white tip and the outer pair of back stripes are generally wider.

The Rio Grande Spotted Skunk (*Spilogale leucoparia*) inhabits the arid regions of western Texas and southern New Mexico west to central Arizona and south into Mexico. It has more than ordinary white, with broader stripes and larger spots.

The Canyon Spotted Skunk (*Spilogale gracilis gracilis*) is found in northern Arizona and the desert ranges of southern California, south into Mexico. It is similar to Rio Grande, except smaller and more slender.

The Great Basin Spotted Skunk (*Spilogale gracilis saxatilis*) ranges through western Colorado, Utah, northern Nevada, southern Idaho, eastern Oregon and northeastern California. It is somewhat larger than the Canyon variety, without outside back-stripes.

The Rocky Mountain Spotted Skunk (*Spilogale tenuis*) is found along the eastern slope of the Rocky Mountains in Colorado and northern New Mexico. Has a narrow side back-stripe; white patch on forehead, and end third of tail white. It is large in size.

The Chihuahua Spotted Skunk (*Spilogale ambigua*) is found

in central Arizona south into Mexico. It has broad white side back-stripes and white bands on thighs.

The Arizona Spotted Skunk (*Spilogale arizonae arizonae*) ranges through central and southern Arizona, southwestern New Mexico and south into Mexico. It has broad white side back-stripes and much white on tail.

The California Spotted Skunk (*Spilogale phenax phenax*) ranges through most of California, except extreme northern and desert regions. It is similar to the type variety except for shorter tail; large white spots on forehead and front of ear; white, curved patch on base of tail; and much white on end extending further back on lower side.

The Oregon Spotted Skunk (*Spilogale phenax latifrons*) is found in the coastal region of Oregon and northern California. It is comparatively small, black and with narrower white stripes and less white on other parts.

The Puget Sound Spotted Skunk (*Spilogale phenax olympica*) ranges through the Olympic Peninsula and the shores of Puget Sound, northward into British Columbia. It is similar to the Oregon variety; except with shorter tail and longer white spot on front of head

As an indication of the economic value of skunks in the trapping business, the latest official records on those States filing reports show well over a million skins of the large striped skunk for the one season, and Canada lists over two hundred thousand. The latest report shows Kansas as the No. 1 skunk State with 171,-807; Texas, 121,573; and Pennsylvania with 103,207; although an examination of records covering the past several years shows a grand total of more skunks taken in Pennsylvania than any other state—255,439 for 1941 is apparently the all time record. What an aromatic party they could have stirred up, if they had all gotten together and done something about it! These were all the large striped skunk, which are of much more economic importance than the little spotted skunk. In only one state in the U.S.A. do the latest records show a larger catch of these than larger relative. In Iowa, during the 1945-46 season a total of 44,827 spotted skunks were reported taken, against 30,755 of the big striped skunk. The last four annual reports for Iowa show the small variety far in excess of the big ones, although this is the only district where this is the case.

The little striped skunk is often called a "civet cat," but this is a mistake, for this name correctly belongs to an Old World animal in no way resembling our own perfume kitty and should not be applied to any creature inhabiting this continent.

The polecat is found in various haunts, although it prefers a more rugged country than its larger cousin. Rocky canyons, cliffs and broken country, as well as forest areas, are favorite spots for the polecat; and they are far greater travelers than skunks. While the latter are more apt to be found around clearings and pastures, deserted old buildings, brush piles and broken country near to the border of woodlands. Dry ravines are also desirable spots to find them. In some sections, however, they are found in quite open prairie country.

They both like holes in the ground, although the skunk is the best digger; and they both prefer to appropriate the hole which some other animal has dug.

The young are generally born in late April or May; and the skunk brings forth as many as ten to a litter, while the polecat seldom has more than six. The average in both cases is about five.

The food of both varieties consists mainly of insects, beetles and grasshoppers, although they will devour small animals, birds, eggs, lizards and occasionally fruit; and poultry is a favorite dish, especially of the larger skunks.

In their daily habits the polecats and skunks are quite different. The former is almost entirely nocturnal, being normally very seldom seen during the daytime; but the skunk may be seen at most any time although it too is most active at night.

Neither variety, because of their odoriferous means of self-protection, have but very few natural enemies. The great horned owl seems to be the most oblivious to their offense and includes both of them on his menu. The bobcat also makes an occasional meal on them; but most carnivorous animals have to be pretty desperate for something to eat to go for them. But the old-time Indians, who called the skunk "peshes piupiu (pronounced something like "peaches phew phew"!), is known to have eaten skunk. Possibly it made him more inclined to go scalp hunting.

Although both skunks and polecats are found in districts where winter brings some pretty frigid weather, they do not really hibernate. They become very fat in the fall, however, and use excellent judgment in spending considerable time inside their dens and various protected haunts during particularly cold weather.

Many trappers use the "cubby" as a method of catching skunk. In fact, the cubby is used in the trapping of most varieties of our fur-bearing animals, whether it is in the deep South or the far North. The principle is always pretty much the same, for the cubby is simply a miniature shed with the front end wide open. They can be built by pushing two rows of parallel sticks into the ground, using a tree, bank or rock for the back and covering the top with sticks, brush or a flat rock. Or, the walls and roof can be made of slabs of rock. The natural recess in a rocky ledge or the stump of an old tree can be made into a cubby. In every instance the materials used should be natural to the surroundings. They can even be constructed on top of many feet of snow. The bait is of course placed at the back and the trap, or traps, set at the entrance.

Skunks and polecats are comparatively easy to trap. The difficulty and skill comes after they are caught. If the location permits concealment without great disturbance, the trap can be set in front of the den—covered with a sprinkling of dead grass. Properly constructed baited sets or cubbies, in the vicinity of dens, generally prove more satisfactory. These baited sets are best when you can take advantage of natural locations, such as a cubby in the rock formation or the hollow base of a tree, so arranged that the animal must step on the trap in order to get to the bait. Sets should be selected, or covered, to avoid crows, blue jays or other birds from stealing the bait or springing the trap; and be sure the entrance is not much wider than the trap when it is set in position. The bait can be chicken heads or entrails; smelly meat scraps; or fish oil scent, made as follows: 1 quart fish oil (either home made or commercial): 1 ounce oil of rodium: 1 ounce oil anise; ½ ounce pulverized asafetida—mixed together in a bottle and shaken well before using. A small quantity of this sprinkled on your baited cubbies will excite the curiosity of skunks and most meat-eating fur-bearing animals and cause them to investigate your set.

These animals have a habit of chewing their foot off underneath the jaws of the trap and then pulling out to escape in a crippled condition. While they may recover, this should be avoided by the trapper. Double-jawed traps prevent this—or visit your traps often.

The setting of traps in the entrance of animal dens is prohibited by law in some states—and such sets are somewhat of an amateur's method, anyhow. There is the additional disadvantage that such sets are as apt to catch cottontail rabbits as skunks. The bunnies are at trapping time protected by game laws throughout the eastern states; and they have a habit of sharing the same dens with skunks. It is not necessary to set traps at or in the entrance to dens to catch skunks. Just select a nearby rock cavity or hollow base of a stump and make a baited set. Or, if there is no natural place to do this, build a cubby for the purpose. Examine the ground around a den that is occupied and you will find one or more trails made by the animals in their regular trips from and to their homes; which can be followed a short distance away, to make your set. By this method you will catch more skunks, in the long run, than setting traps right in the entrance, and not waste your chances on the bunnies.

It is comparatively easy to determine whether a den is being used or not. In the fall, you will find a certain amount of grass, leaves etc., which the animals have dropped during the process of carrying it inside to make the den room more comfortable for cold winter days. They will rake this material inside from as near at hand as possible and sometimes make quite a mess in doing so. The more extensive the raked area is, the more skunks you can figure are living there.

Fall is a good time to locate dens and plan your later trapping program. At this time both skunks and polecats feed on bugs, mice, etc., which they find in meadows or other open sections of their territory. An experienced trapper can quickly identify the places where they have been digging—and this is an indication that one or more dens are not very far away. When a den is located, do the necessary preliminary clearing out or re-arrange-ment of the crevices or stumps which will later be used for your sets.

A hollow log lying on the ground is another good place to make a set. Put the bait inside—it can be chicken entrails, fish, rabbit, etc., and it does not have to be fresh. The traps are, of course, set at each entrance. Place them just outside, or just inside, and cover lightly with dry grass or a few leaves.

The "rock" garden set can be used where there is much open ground and few places for cubby type of locations. In the fall, or as long before trapping time as possible, place either large or small rocks in piles on the ground in such a way that there are two or three entrances to the central opening. The openings should not be more than eight or ten inches, or just a convenient width for a skunk to walk into the trap that will be set there. When ready to use, place the bait in the center and a trap set in each entrance. Attach each trap to a drag, rather than a stake, so that a trapped skunk will get away from the set and increase your chances for another catch during the same period.

The skunk has proved to be more of a pest than a prize to many a fox trapper—for they seem to have a bad habit of getting into (and spoiling) the best of fox sets. If the skunk has not ruined such a set by clawing and biting, before you find him, he is pretty sure to do so with other ways and means at his disposal before you can kill him and complete the task at hand. The best advice to the fox trapper whose trapping grounds are inhabited with skunks, is to try to get rid of these before you go after the more mild pelts.

It is possible to kill a trapped skunk without the usual obnoxious pollution—but this is a trapper's art. The surest way is by drowning; but this is generally very difficult. Shooting invariably results in a stench-drenched pelt, unless the spinal cord is cut. If the tail can be kept down, the animal is defenseless, but in this the risk is great. Breaking the back, and thus eliminating muscular control over the glands, before discharge is made, is the best method. In any event, the amateur is sure to have some interesting experiences before he becomes an expert. But that's part of the fun; and next to the muskrat, these animals provide most of the fur income throughout rural United States.

A method used by some trappers is to carry with them an eight-to ten-foot pole to the end of which is attached about a two- to three-foot piece of annealed No. 15 or 16 wire with a slip noose at the end. The latter is slipped over the head of a trapped skunk or polecat, and with a quick jerk backwards and upwards the animal is lifted as high in the air as the trap chain will permit; and there held until he is strangled. This can often be accomplished without any discharge; and if there is, it is downward to the ground and not as dangerous as might be.

The skunk is about 75 percent beneficial to the farmer, because of his destruction of insect pests and other farmer enemies. His one depredation is upon poultry and eggs; but on the average farm, the good he does outweighs the damage. And in spite of his offensiveness, the great amount of money which he annually brings to trappers makes him well worth the effort and inconvenience which he sometimes causes.

The value of all furs is to a large degree influenced by the current styles which are in popularity; but, as a general rule, the skunk pelts with the least white bring the highest price on the market.

CHAPTER VII

THE MINK

THE mink is probably our most valuable fur-bearing animal. While not the most numerous, it is found from Arctic Alaska to Florida and from Labrador to Texas; is comparatively plentiful in the best parts of its natural range; is not particularly difficult to trap; and its skin consistently commands a high price. The catch in the U.S. brings in well over ten million dollars anually to trappers. That's a lot of folding money in any language.

Not only is the mink a prize peltry for the trapper, but individually they are also mighty interesting little fellows. Of all our fur bearers they are undoubtedly the most versatile and resourceful, and endowed with an unusual amount of dexterity in the matter of self-preservation and procuring a living. They are equally at home on land and in the water; can go up a tree like a squirrel; disappear in the grass like a field mouse; out-run or out-dodge practically all of their natural enemies of the land or the air; and when occasion necessitates they can fight like a demon. A trapped mink is often a red-eyed wild rage of fury. Whether it is a fox, dog, wildcat, otter or owl which launches the attack, the little mink is generally quite capable of taking care of himself, no matter where the attack takes place. In the water they can swim with such skill that fish are a regular item on their menu; on the ground they frequently capture rabbits for food; and birds also provide a common meal. Although their legs are short, they are so supple and lithe that the entire length of their long body is activitated in producing their incredible swiftness. They can even travel across glare ice with such ease and grace that it sometimes seems they are wearing tiny skates. To watch a smart old mink after a grouse is a sight worth spending the time. Even if the bird knows that it is being pursued, the skill and persistence of the stalking mink is something to be admired.

The young are born in April or May and the average litter is generally five or six.

There are eleven scientifically recognized varieties of the Mink (*Mustela vison* and related forms), of which the Eastern or Little Black Mink is considered the type form. This one normally has a body measurement of around twenty-four inches, with the tail vertebrae adding about eight inches in length. A large male will weigh around two pounds, sometimes a little more; while females will tip the scales at little more than one pound ten ounces. Both sexes are colored alike, with no seasonal variation. The back or upperparts are generally of a uniform dark brown, glossy and rich in appearance, slightly darker along the middle of the back and tail while the underparts are generally but slightly lighter, with white or yellow on the chin and occasionally similar spots elsewhere on the throat or belly. This variety ranges through eastern Canada, west to Hudson's Bay; south into the Catskill Mountains in New York and into northern Pennsylvania; and in the coastal regions south into New Brunswick.

The Common Mink (*Mustela vison mink*) is found in the eastern United States from the coast of New England south to North Carolina and through the interior to central Georgia and Alabama; and westward through southern Pennsylvania and Ohio to Missouri and northeastern Texas. This variety is slightly larger than the Eastern Mink and generally a little darker in color.

The Florida Mink (*Mustela vison lutensis*) inhabits the coastal regions of the southeastern States from South Carolina into Florida. It is smaller than either of the above and pale reddish brown to russet clay in color.

The Southern Mink (*Mustela vison vulgivaga*) inhabits the coastal regions of Louisiana and Mississippi, north in the Missis-

MINK

RUNNING TRACKS

12"

HIND

FORE

THE PASSAGEWAY SET

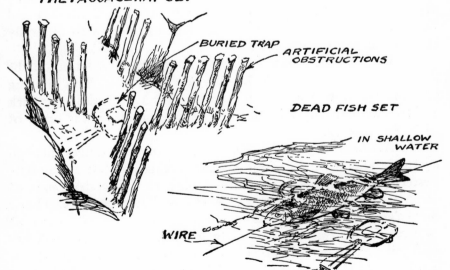

BURIED TRAP ARTIFICIAL OBSTRUCTIONS

DEAD FISH SET

IN SHALLOW WATER

WIRE

sippi River bottoms to northern Louisiana. It is slightly larger than the Florida variety but darker; the color being uniform lustrous light brown with end of tail dark, and white spot on chin and throat.

The Mississippi Valley Mink (*Mustela vison letifera*) is found from northern Missouri and southern Kansas north to northern Illinois and South Dakota. This is the largest of the mink yet described, the males ranging to twenty-six inches or more in body length, with an additional nine to ten inch tail vertebrae. It is light brown in color, inclined to have more white on throat and on breast.

The Hudson Bay Mink (*Mustela vison lacustris*) ranges through the interior of Canada from the western shore of Hudson's Bay westward to Great Bear Lake, and south through Manitoba, Saskatchewan to Alberta to southern North Dakota. This variety is inclined to be even larger than the Mississippi Valley Mink; and it is dark chocolate-brown in color, with the belly a little lighter and considerable white on chin, breast and sometimes between hind legs.

The Western or Pacific Mink (*Mustela vison energumenos*) is found from northern British Columbia south through the Rocky Mountains and the Sierra Nevada Mountains into California and New Mexico. It is a small mink but dark in color, with generally but a small white spot on chin.

The Kenai Mink (*Mustela vison melampeplus*) is found on the Kenai Peninsula and Cook Inlet region in Alaska. This is a big mink, larger even than the Hudson Bay Mink. It is also very dark in color, without any reddish tinge. Many consider it the finest of all in fur quality.

The Alaska or Big Mink (*Mustela vison ingens*) ranges through northern, western and central Alaska; northern Yukon and northwestern Mackenzie River country; south to the western part of the Alaska Peninsula and to the Anderson River country. This is the largest of all the American minks, attaining a length of twenty-nine to thirty inches body length, plus a seven to eight-inch tail vertebrae. It has a three-inch hind foot. Only in color is it inferior to the Kenai variety, and this is particularly true when taken in the coastal regions, especially on the Alaska Peninsula, where the fur is not only lighter but also somewhat coarser in texture.

The Island Mink (*Mustela vison nesolestes*) is found only on the Alexander Archipelago, Alaska. This one is considerably smaller than the other two Alaskan varieties; somewhat lighter in color and is inclined to have more white on it than any of the other American minks, even on the inner parts of the fore legs and abdomen.

The California Mink (*Mustela vison aestuarina*) is found in the lowlands of west-central California. It is a comparatively small mink, pale in color and pelage not so heavy as other varieties.

The mink, as a whole, belongs to the same scientific family as the weasels, martens, wolverines, badgers and skunks. All of these, to a varying degree, have the scent glands for which the skunks are so notorious. In the minks, this is primarily a sex attraction; and while they are not capable of any proficient use of this unusual equipment with which Dame Nature has provided them, many trappers consider the "musk" of the mink, when contacted in strongly unadulterated potions, more objectionable even than that of their more odoriferous cousins the skunks. But spending, as they do, so much of their time in the water, the minks do not normally carry much of the odor about with them.

The greatest abundance of mink in North America, surprising as it may seem to many, is apparently in the State of Louisiana. According to the records compiled by the U.S. Fish and Wild Life Service, 168,598 mink were caught there during the 1945-46 trapping season. The number was of course larger than that, because this figure represents only those pelts which were reported to the authorities. The second highest figure for the same period was 95,782 for the State of Minnesota; nearby Michigan produced 53,400; Iowa, 48,145; Texas, 35,592; Alaska, 31,339; Florida, 6,560. This gives a comprehensive idea, at a glance, of the wide relative distribution of this important fur bearer.

Mink taken in the higher altitudes of the Appalachian Range and north of the latitude of the Mason and Dixon Line generally have a higher market value than those caught farther south; although they all find a ready sale at good prices.

Trapping methods vary to some extent in the extremes of this fur bearer's habitat. After all, there is a lot of difference between the humid Louisiana marshes and Alaska at sixty degrees below zero!

In the marshes of Louisiana and along the Sabine River in eastern Texas a good many mink are caught in regular muskrat sets. But the smart muskrat trapper, when he finds fresh mink signs on his line, will make a regular mink set. The mink is not only valuable, but they are inclined to prey on muskrats. An old mink will kill a good many muskrats if he really develops a taste for them. The mink habitually travel around the edges of the wet marshes and follow the miles of ditches that cut through many of the marshes. These places are always good hunting grounds to find frogs and other foods liked by mink, and they will stop to investigate any hole or muskrat workings. A fish bait, with some sprinkling of fish oil and a few drops of the fluid from the scent glands of a mink added, is sure to attract his attention and cause a close investigation which should add his pelt to your catch. Most mink in this sort of terrain however, are taken in blind sets.

Where any spring flows or a small stream enters a much larger stream, is an ideal place to make a blind set. Most mink, when traveling along a stream, will go up these small off-shoots at least a short distance and then cross back overland to the main stream again. Select a suitable place near the mouth and place obstructions made of rocks or piles or sticks in such a manner as to leave only one inviting place for the mink to pass through. If you can find such a natural passageway, so much the better. Place your trap, carefully concealed, in this opening. If the side stream is shallow or the bank broad, you can construct a barrier by pushing dead sticks into the bottom, close enough together so that the mink cannot get through. Leave an opening four or five inches wide at the most suitable place and conceal your trap there. Shallow water a couple inches deep makes a good set. If it is near deeper water, into which you can run a sliding wire so he will drown, so much the better. Do not use scent or bait for this set. It is particularly good in the fall, when the mink are doing considerable traveling and they still can find food such as frogs, crayfish and snakes along the little feeder-streams. Remember that, the mink is strictly carnivorous in its feeding habits. Its diet also consists of fish, mice, muskrats, rabbits, other small animals and birds, and this fine little fur bearer is seldom found very far from water. The banks of creeks where there is good cover of thick trees or brush is their favorite haunt. They only travel through the woods when crossing from one body of water to another. They den in the ground in old muskrat burrows, rock bluffs, and sometimes in hollow logs—but never very far from water.

The mink is a great traveler, following the banks of streams and lakes for long distances, in the night. Like most all other wild animals, he habitually follows the same route at periodical intervals, unless radically disturbed in this routine. The female mink usually covers its regular route of travel, in its hunting quest for food, every other night. The male is apt to make longer trips and may not cover the same route more than once a week. In these travels they invariably visit certain spots on each and every trip. These favorite places may be a deserted muskrat den, a pile of driftwood, hollow log or tree, rock bluff den, or the bottom of a narrow stream bed. The wise trapper will acquaint himself with the location of these particular places and make his trap sets in or near to them. When there is snow on the ground, these spots are quite easy to locate.

Mink will also as a rule enter and leave the water at the same place. By careful observation, even when there is no snow on the ground, these places can be located by signs; and they make excellent places for sets. The trap should be placed in about three inches of water, with the chain drawn out and staked in deep water so the animal will drown.

During the fall trapping activities, in the colder regions, you should anticipate where the mink will visit during midwinter. They will travel on the banks through the snow and if the snow is deep they will burrow under it, sometimes for considerable distances, although they do not always travel repeatedly in the same tracks. They will generally, however, make repeat visits to washed out cavities under the roots of big trees, old hollow logs near the stream, rock cavities, abandoned muskrat holes and pools of dead water where fish such as suckers congregate to spend the winter. They will also have runways under the ice where it is propped up against the bank. All of such regularly visited places are good for baited or blind sets, according to the situation. Most such places have the additional advantage that your trap will be sheltered from the snow. You can quite easily locate the places where he goes under or comes out from under the ice. If these provide an opportunity of placing the trap in shallow water, so much the better. Incidentally, any cheap grade of canned salmon is a good bait for winter; and adding some strong fish oil or mink scent makes it even better. And for a cubby set, to sprinkle some light colored chicken or duck feathers over or around the normal bait will excite their curiosity and contribute to the chances of a catch.

Trapping mink in the northern districts in midwinter has many problems and is considerably more difficult than where the water is open and the ground not frozen. Snow, thaws, freezing, sub-zero conditions makes the mere problem of keeping traps in working order a major one. But if the coldest weather is constant, and not mild one day and freezing another, it presents less difficulties. At best it is hard work, although the cold climate trapper is paid extra dividends for his pelts.

Bait sets and scents are not as effective in low temperature weather as they are in mild. A frozen bait does not give off the attractive lure that it does otherwise; and while the scents do not work as effectively until late in the season when mating begins, they never do any harm.

Blind sets are generally considered more effective for mink in cold climates. This means that the trapper has to know his game that much better and to a larger degree calls upon the individual's ingenuity in analyzing each situation as he finds it. The real secret to making blind sets is: first, to anticipate just where the game will pass; second, cleverly crowding him in to pass through a narrow given spot, by placing obstructions to effect this; and third, placing the trap where he will unwittingly step into it.

As to the proper trap to use for mink, there is some difference of opinion among expert trappers. The No. 1½ or the No. 1½ D Coil Spring; the No. 1½ or No. 2 Long Spring; or the No. 1½ Jump are all used extensively. Some insist on the double-jawed trap, to prevent loss of mink that chew off their feet underneath the jaw and pull out.

Under certain conditions a whole fish makes an excellent set for mink. It requires running water in a shallow stream where the water will not freeze. Run a wire through the entire length of the fish and fasten it securely in the stream not far from the shore. If the top fin shows above the surface, so much the better. Then place a trap on either side of the fish. If this set is well made and fresh fish are used, there are few mink that will resist going to it.

The freshly skinned carcass of a muskrat is also a good bait in winter when the mink have to do more hunting for their suppers. It can be placed in any natural grotto among rocks or in an old dead stump along the shore. Under overhanging banks there is often sheltered dry places which make good sets.

A good general rule for trapping is to make and leave as few unnatural signs of disturbance as possible. The fewer signs you leave behind the better and no trapper can be too careful about this. Learn to make your sets quickly, but carefully, and with the least possible disarrangement of the location. Even a cubby should be made to blend into the background and appear a natural part of its surroundings. If it stands out like a "sore thumb," it's a poor cubby. And it is a worthwhile added precaution to take along a tin cup for the purpose of washing away all foreign odors after the trap is in place.

A matter of general advice on mink baits is to use only fresh meat—whether muskrat, chicken parts, fish, porcupine or rabbit. Stale or over-ripe bait is practically worthless for mink.

To make scent for mink trapping, place the musk glands of several mink in about two ounces of fish oil and let stand. The fish oil is made by cutting any fatty fish, such as trout or salmon, into small pieces and let stand in a clean glass jar in the warm sun, until the oil can be poured off. The musk from the scent glands of beaver or muskrat is also effective for mink.

Mink should be case-skinned, with the feet and claws left on. The skins are not particularly difficult to handle because they have a tendency to come clean without retaining any great amount of fat, and there is not the usual danger of spoilage if the tail is not split after the tail vertebrae is pulled out. Some buyers however, recommend splitting the tail. The skin should be stretched flesh side out, although it can be reversed after thoroughly drying on the stretcher. Most experienced trappers prefer the patented wire stretchers because they can be adjusted for size. If you are going to make your own wooden stretcher boards, they should be ¼ to ⅜ inch; at least 36 inches in length; and tapering from 4½ inches at the base to 3¼ inches at the shoulder; and sandpapered smooth. Adjustable boards are used by many trappers (either spreading or with tongue inserted), but when using these be careful not to unduly stretch the green skin when it is put on.

In many sections of the country trappers would take a lot more mink if it were not for the pollution of our streams. The disappearance of the mink from many of his former favorite haunts is because so many of their favorite breeding streams have been so polluted by mine water and other industrial waste that no aquatic life exists; therefore the mink cannot exist there, as they depend almost entirely on such fish as suckers, chubs and other slow-moving fish, at least during the breeding and rearing season. Little evidence is found of their being very destructive to trout. Examination of their dining places invariably shows only the scales of suckers or other coarse fish. The same is also true of the otter, which have also been driven from most of their former favorite breeding places by the pollution of our streams. This is the most serious problem confronting our fur bearer conservationists today.

CHAPTER VIII

THE WEASEL

INCH for inch and ounce for ounce, the little weasel is the blood-thirsty fightenest animal on this continent and probably all the earth. Slender and almost fragile in appearance though he may appear, the size of the foe means nothing to him; and he is one of the few creatures that kills for the sheer lust of killing. It surely must be that the little weasel is the reincarnation of some anciently condemned demon personality. But they have a beautiful little pelt, which has for centuries been the favored choice of kings, princes and their most discriminating consorts. It is the sadistic little "ermine" that always shines brightest at the most regal Old World court ceremonies, among the dowager first-nighters at the Opera, or the glitter and glare of the sun-light arcs at a Hollywood premiere. With all its lust and elegance, the little weasel has a lot to commend it.

The Weasel (*Mustela cicognani* and related forms) is closely related to the Mink, as can be seen from their Latin name; and there are thirty-five scientifically recognized varieties, not including the Black-footed Ferret, which is really a member of the same family. There is a marked difference between many of these varieties, particularly in size—far more so than among the different scientific varieties of most of our fur bearers. The smallest known variety is the Plains Least Weasel, found only in Nebraska, and the male having a total body length of 7½". The largest variety is the New Mexico Bridled Weasel, found in the Mesilla Valley of New Mexico and having a body length of 20" and tail vertebrae 8" in length. Most of the variations in all these different varieties, however, are purely scientific, such as the construction of the head, teeth and other things which are quite important to scientists but of little consequence to the trappers. But for the general information of those interested, here very briefly is the whole list. You can find your own variety in the list.

The Bonaparte Weasel (*Mustela cicognani cicognani*) is the type form. Its body measurements are about eleven inches, plus a tail vertebrae about three and a half inches in length. The female is about two inches shorter. Summer pelage is chocolate brown, somewhat darker on top of head; with underparts yellowish. In winter it is all white except for black top of tail and yellowish tinge on underparts. Its range extends across northern North America from Labrador and New England to the Pacific Coast of southeastern Alaska and south in the Rocky Mountains to Colorado.

The Newfoundland Weasel (*Mustela cicognani mortignea*) is found only in Newfoundland. Somewhat larger than Bonaparte (13").

The Richardson Weasel (*Mustela cicognani richardsoni*) ranges from Hudson's Bay to interior of Alaska and northern British Columbia. Larger than either of the above (15½").

The Juneau Weasel (*Mustela cicognani alascensis*) is found in a limited area around Juneau, Alaska on the mainland. Medium in size.

The Small-eared Weasel (*Mustela microtis*) is found only in the vicinity of Shesby, British Columbia. Ears very small. (11¾" body.)

The Puget Sound Weasel (*Mustela streatori streatori*) ranges in the coastal regions of Puget Sound, south through Washington and Oregon (11").

The Dwarf Weasel (*Mustela streatori leptus*) is found in the Rocky Mountains from Alberta south into Colorado. Very small, 9¾" body, 2½" tail vertebrae. Very white without yellow tinge and only tip of tail black.

WEASEL

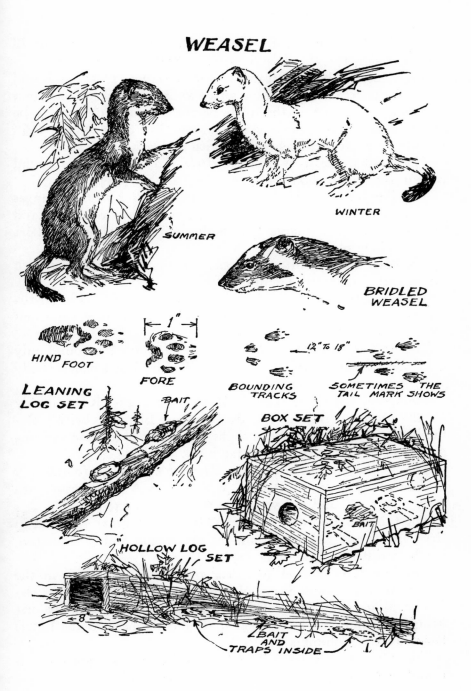

SUMMER

WINTER

BRIDLED WEASEL

HIND FOOT

1"

FORE

BOUNDING TRACKS

12" TO 18"

SOMETIMES THE TAIL MARK SHOWS

LEANING LOG SET

BAIT

BOX SET

BAIT

"HOLLOW LOG SET

8

BAIT AND TRAPS INSIDE

The Little Weasel (*Mustela muricus*) is found only in El Dorado County, California. Somewhat smaller than Dwarf.

The Least or Bangs Weasel (*Mustela rixosa rixosa*) is found over a large area from Hudson's Bay to St. Michaels on the coast of Alaska, south to northern Minnesota. By some claimed to be the smallest of the weasels. Averages less than 8″ body and 1½″ tail vertebrae. It is entirely white, with no black tip on tail.

The Alaskan Least Weasel (*Mustela rixosa eskimo*) is found only in the region about Point Barrow, Alaska. (11¼″).

The Tundra or Arctic Weasel (*Mustela arctica arctica*) ranges through a considerable area along the Arctic coast of Alaska and western Canada. It is large (16″ body) with comparatively short tail with long black tip.

The Polar Weasel (*Mustela arctica polaris*) is found in northern Greenland. Similar to Tundra.

The Greenland Weasel (*Mustela audax*) is also found in northern Greenland, but smaller and with other anatomical variations of little importance to trappers.

The Kodiak Island Weasel (*Mustela kodiacensis*) is found only on Kodiak Island, Alaska. Resembles Tundra but smaller (body 12¾″).

The Queen Charlotte Weasel (*Mustela haidarum*) is found only on the Queen Charlotte Islands (Graham Islands), British Columbia. In winter white with slight orange tinge on rear and underparts and more than half of tail black (body 11½″).

The Washington Weasel (*Mustela washingtoni*) is found only in the vicinity of Mount Adams, Washington. A large weasel with body about 16″ and tail vertebrae 6″; females 14½″.

The Cascade Mountain Weasel (*Mustela saturata*) is found in the Cascade and Siskiyu Mountains of Oregon and Washington, north into British Columbia (17″).

The Mountain Weasel (*Mustela arizonensis*) is found in the Rocky Mountains and Sierra Nevadas (15½″).

The Mountain Long-tailed Weasel (*Mustela longicauda oribasus*) is found only in the region around the head of the Kettle River, British Columbia (15½″).

The Oregon Weasel (*Mustela xanthogenys oregonensis*) is found in the Rogue River Valley, Oregon (18″).

The California Weasel (*Mustela xanthogenys xanthogenys*) is found in the Sierra Nevada Mountains of California (16").

The Redwoods Weasel (*Mustela xanthogenys munda*) ranges along the coastal regions of California. In winter the upperparts are a dark russet, underparts deep orange. In summer darker above and paler underneath (15").

The Plains Least Weasel (*Mustela campestris*) is found only in Cumming County, Nebraska. Smallest of the weasels; body of male 7½" with tail vertebrae 3⅓".

The Long-tailed Weasel (*Mustela longicauda longicauda*) ranges over the great plains from Kansas northward into Canada. A large variety, body 18", tail vertebrae 6½".

The Northern Long-tailed Weasel (*Mustela occisor*) taken only near Bucksport, Maine. Same size as Long-tailed variety, except with a longer tail.

The Black Hills Weasel (*Mustela alleni*) is found in the Black Hills, South Dakota (15").

The Minnesota Weasel (*Mustela longicauda spadix*) is found in the timber areas of Minnesota. A large weasel (18") with long tail (6½").

The Missouri Weasel (*Mustela primulina*) is found only in Jasper County, Missouri (13").

The Alleghenian Least Weasel (*Mustela allegheniensis*) is found in the Allegheny Mountains, Pennsylvania. In winter entirely white. Very small, body 8", tail vertebrae 1".

The Bridled Weasel (*Mustela frenata frenata*) is found in southern Texas south into Mexico. Male body length 19½" with tail vertebrae 7¾"; females, 17½" and 7½". It gets its name from conspicuous white markings on the head which gives the appearance of wearing a bridle. It does not turn white in winter.

The New Mexico Bridled Weasel (*Mustela frenata neomexicana*) is found in the Mesilla Valley of New Mexico. Resembles Bridled except with more white on head. This is the largest of all of the weasels. Male body length 20" with tail vertebrae 8". Its hind foot is 2" long.

The New York Weasel (*Mustela noveboracensis noveboracensis*) is found in eastern United States from southern Maine to North Carolina and west to Illinois. In the northern part of its range it turns white in winter, but not in the southern part. Tail long and bushy, with black tip nearly half the length of tail (13⅓").

The Southern Weasel (*Mustela noveboracensis notia*) is found from the District of Columbia south into North Carolina (17").

The Florida Weasel (*Mustela pensinsulae peninsulae*) ranges through Florida. Large, but of course does not turn white in winter.

The Alabama Weasel (*Mustela peninsulae olivacea*) is found in central Alabama. Similar to Florida variety.

The Black-footed Ferret (*Mustela nigripes*) ranges over the great plains from western North Dakota and northern Montana south to Texas. Total length of body 23" and tail vertebrae 5¼" Upperparts pale buffy yellow, with a sprinkling of brown hairs on back; underparts cream colored; feet black; broad black band across eyes like a mask; short tail, with blackish tip; known to kill prairie dogs.

The greatest abundance of weasels in the United States, as indicated from the official records of skins reported for the 1945-56 trapping season was in Minnesota, where 85,125 were tabulated. Next came Michigan with 48,501; Wisconsin, 10,669; and while North Dakota only reported 5,722 for this last season for which reports have been tabulated, 175,000 were reported for 1940-41. These figures follow the same general pattern for so many of our fur bearers, showing the greatest abundance to be centered in the States around the Great Lakes. The reasons for this probably are because of the abundance of lakes and large timbered areas which form an ideal home of these wild creatures. This is further evidenced by the catch in Canada, where the following numbers of weasel were taken during the 1943-44 trapping season. Saskatchewan, 254,780; Alberta, 180,473; Manitoba, 143,067; Ontario, 69,883; etc. An examination of the records covering the past several years does not show any noticeable decrease in the number of weasels taken.

The weasel is best known for its white winter pelage; but in the southern part of its range where there are no long cold periods of snow, the weasel does not turn white in winter. In the south they maintain the brown and yellow summer pelage throughout the year, instead of turning to white as they do in the northern winters.

With such a variation in size, the weasels naturally have a variable diet. The smaller ones feed on meadow mice and small rodents, while the larger varieties are capable of killing snow-shoe rabbits, prairie-dogs, ptarmigan and other large game birds.

They habitually hunt on the ground, but are not averse to easy tree climbing to make a kill or rob a nest of young birds. They are one of the most restless and seemingly most nervous of all creatures; possessed of exceptionally keen sense of smell, sight and hearing; are persistent hunters; and are such desperate killers that they are undoubtedly considered slinking devils to all small mammals and ground-nesting birds who inhabit their haunts. They are most active at night, but frequently hunt during the day, and they are active throughout all seasons of the year, no matter how severe the winter may be.

According to many authorities the favorite food of all the weasels is warm blood, sucked from the neck or base of the skull of the victims it kills; and they kill not only for food, but apparently for the sheer pleasure of doing so. There are records of a single weasel killing as many as forty chickens in a single night. Very often, however, the good that is done by the weasel outweigh his depredations, by the large number of mice he kills. One weasel will do more good in this respect in a farmer's barn, than three or four ordinary cats. But on the whole he is a little desperado.

Six to eight young are born to a litter.

Weasels are exceedingly curious little creatures. This characteristic, coupled with a defiant boldness, sometimes causes them to appear almost foolhardy. They frequently come right into a trapper's cabin at night in the north woods, if there is a hole of sufficient size in the floor; and if carefully encouraged, they will even become so tame, after a few visits, that they will take bits of meat out of one's fingers. And when one is found in the woods it can often be attracted by a squeak or whistle. Even after it has disappeared in a pile of logs or a rock-pile it can often be coaxed out again to investigate the sounds you make.

Because of their thin body and short legs the weasel can pursue the small rodents upon which it preys, even into their own burrows and holes among the rocks, as well as along their narrow runways through the grass. Not only do these little killers have the most highly developed hunting sense, but it is apparent that they have a sense of smell which enables them to trail their game like a hound dog on the trail of a fox or a 'coon. And once they set out to get a victim, it seldom escapes. When game is plentiful they are content to suck only the warm blood, although in very cold weather or during periods of scarcity of food, they have been known not only to eat the flesh of their victims, but *cache* it as a provision for future feeding. Their favorite menu is the white-footed mouse. They generally kill by forcing their hypodermic-like teeth through the skull and into the brain. The blood is sucked through the large veins in the neck; and after that, if they are so inclined, they generally eat the brains. If still hungry, and disinclined to stalk and kill again (which is seldom the case) they eat the flesh, turning back the skin as they go, leaving it turned inside out with the feet and tail attached.

In many sections of the country the weasel is the personification of a bad ghost to most rabbits, particularly in winter. The bunnies will generally make a very hasty race for the wide open spaces the moment they become aware of a weasel on their trail. Normal rabbits seek the thick undergrowth for self-protection— but not from a weasel. The little white killer is more adept at racing through the thick stuff than the best rabbit, whose only chance is in the open, where the weasel will seldom follow him.

In more settled districts the weasel has a liking for old stone fences, overgrown with weeds. These are always good hunting grounds for mice. They also like areas grown up thickly with growths of young pine and birch, blackberry vines and briars. If such areas are interspersed with piles of rocks or broken hedges, they like it even more. For their homes they like the hollow roots of old trees, dead stumps with holes running into the ground, small caves in rocky ledges and they are not averse to appropriating the burrows of ground-squirrels after the occupants have been murdered.

When a weasel really sets out to go places he does so with gliding leaps that often take him several yards at a bound, the hind feet following directly in back of the front ones. They are great travelers, sometimes covering two or three miles in a single night; and frequently these travels keep them away from "home" for a week or more. The males are generally greater travelers than females.

Weasels are quite easily trapped, as they walk into a trap with apparent disregard. Although they prefer to kill their own food, they can be enticed into a cubby with the use of most any bloody scraps of meat or even parts of the carcass of their own kind.

The trap generally used is the No. O or the No. 1. Some trappers even use an ordinary house rat trap of the wooden platform and spring variety.

It is comparatively easy to identify a rabbit that has been killed by a weasel, and if the little killer has indulged in more than just warm blood, the chances are that he will return again to feast on the flesh. Being small, they do not require a great amount of flesh to satisfy their satanic appetites. Usually, after a rabbit is killed, they suck the blood and eat a small portion of the head and neck; then leave the carcass right where the kill was made. If it is right out in the open, it can be dragged to one side where there is some growth or other surrounding in which you can place some obstruction on three sides of it and thus compel the weasel, when he returns, to approach it where the trap is set.

Weasels seem to have a considerable disdain for traps—just as they do for nearly everything else in their world. There is no doubt that a carefully concealed trap will take far more weasels than one that is even partly concealed. Weasels are not dumb; and although they may walk quite blindly into a carelessly set trap, there is still enough instinctive precaution in their make up to cause all of them some times to shy away and some of them always to do so.

Baited sets can be made around old log or brush piles, road culverts or under the edge of an old abandoned building. Most any bloody meat will do—even the freshly skinned carcass of one of their own kind, cut into three or four sections, with a little of the fluid from the weasel's scent glands scattered about, will generally bring results.

The hollow log set, which is so popular as a means of trapping mink, skunk and other fur bearers, is also equally effective on weasel. With the bait in the middle and a trap set at each end, the chances of success are fairly certain if there is any game in the vicinity. Some trappers even make their own "hollow-logs" by nailing strips of one inch boards into elongate three-sided boxes about 7 by 8 inches and 5 or 6 feet long. There should be no bottom to the box, so that the bait, and the traps can be put on the ground. When this box is put in place, it should be camouflaged with whatever helps to make it blend into the setting—grass, brush, leaves or snow.

One of the disadvantages of trapping weasels is that other larger and stronger animals are often caught. If it happens to be a mink, skunk or the like, it not only pulls out of the small trap, but becomes more trap-shy. In view of this, most trappers try to make their weasel sets so that other fur bearers cannot get into them. The most popular set of this nature is a constructed box about 12 inches long and 8 or 10 inches wide and high. Only the bottom is left open, although many trappers put the top or a hinge for lifting to examine the set. In one or both ends of the box a hole about 2 inches in diameter is cut an inch or so from the ground. If there is a good bait inside, and a little scent scattered around, most any weasel will crawl in through the hole. This set has the added advantage, that the caught fur bearer is not torn to pieces by owls. The box should be partly covered or camouflaged as suggested for the longer one.

A good deep snow set is to select a 5- or 6-inch dead log about 6 or 8 feet long. About half way up the log chop out a place to fasten a No. 0 trap. Lean the log against a rock or log pile, old tree or bank at a 45-degree angle or less and with the trap on the top side. Use a bloody bait; and drag it around the general vicinity, leading to the base of the log on which the trap is set; and smear some of the blood up along the log to where the trap is set. Fasten the bait just above the trap. The trap should be sprinkled with dry rotten wood, pine needles or grass.

In skinning a weasel care should be exercised, because the white fur is stained very easily by blood. Also make sure that your stretching boards are carefully smoothed, as the skin of the little weasel is easily damaged. They are always case-skinned and should not be over-stretched when put on the boards.

CHAPTER IX

THE RACCOON

TO THE old-time Sioux Indians the raccoon was known by the name "wica." This same word also signified "a male of the human species," and was used as an adjective prefixed to nouns that have reference to man—as for example, "wicako" means "the human voice." This probably originated from the animal's reputation of being shrewd and knowing. The old expression "as sly as a 'coon" was not restricted to the primitive Indians. This animal's latin name *"lotor,"* which refers to his habit of washing his food, also gives a little preliminary insight into the personality of these creatures.

The Raccoon (*Procyon lotor* and related forms) inhabits most of North America south of about 50° latitude or one hundred to more than five hundred miles north of the U.S.-Canada border. There are seven scientifically recognized varieties:

The Eastern Raccoon (*Procyon lotor lotor*) ranges throughout most of the United States from the Atlantic coastal regions to the Rocky Mountains and from southern Ontario and Manitoba to Florida. This is the type variety. It is a robust omnivorous creature, rather closely related to the bears and with a good many little traits and actions which reminds one of old bruin. His ringed tail and black mask across his eyes is a familiar identification, and the grizzled gray, brown and black pelage of a " 'coon skin coat" is as

durable and practical as it has been popular through many generations, dating back to the days when a 'coon skin cap was as
much the mark of distinction of certain glamorous breeds of
American frontiersmen as the silk top hat is today for swanky
socialites. The average size for an Eastern Raccoon runs around
thirty to thirty-two inches body length plus about a ten-inch tail
vertebrae; and the average male will weigh around fifteen to
eighteen pounds, although now and then an old one will tip the
scales considerably more. This is the smallest of all our raccoons.

The Florida Raccoon (*Procyon lotor elucus*) is found principally in Florida, ranging up into eastern Georgia. It has a longer
tail, more rounded ear and the pelage is far more yellowish in
color, sometimes with a deep orange patch on the shoulders. It is
also larger than the Eastern variety.

The Texas or Brown-footed Raccoon (*Procyon lotor fuscipes*)
ranges through a limited area in southern Texas and south into
Coahuila, Mexico. This is the largest of all North American
'Coons; with a pale gray pelage and black tipped guard hairs, and
the black mask on its face somewhat larger than in other varieties.

The Desert or Pallid Raccoon (*Procyon pallidus*) is found on
the Colorado Desert, in Imperial County and along the Colorado
River as far as Needles. This variety is medium in size; very pale
gray in color, even the hind feet; and with a long slender tail.

The Southwestern or San Diego Raccoon (*Procyon lotor californicus*) ranges over a large part of southwestern California.
This is almost as small as the Eastern variety, although it is very
light in color. In some cases the dark rings on the tail are almost
absent on the underpart.

The California Raccoon (*Procyon lotor psora*) ranges over a
large area in California excepting the northern border and the
southeastern deserts. In color it is yellowish gray mixed with black
on the upperparts and the five to seven dark bands on its tail are
generally broken on the underside.

The Pacific Raccoon (*Procyon lotor pacifica*) ranges over the
northwest coastal region from Puget Sound and the Cascade
Mountains of Washington south into Shasta County, California.
This is a larger 'coon with a comparatively long tail. It is darker
than its neighboring varieties.

RACCOON

LEFT FORE FOOT

3"

RIGHT FORE

LEFT HIND

RIGHT HIND

TRAPS IN SHALLOW WATER

PROTECTING LOG

TRAIL

COVERED TRAP

The usual litter of young varies from three to six, usually born in April or May.

The raccoon is more important economically, as a fur-bearing animal, than many persons surmise, and it provides the principal catch for many trappers. He certainly is grand game, whether taken with traps or an all-night expedition with a couple of good 'coon dogs. He is native to some pretty frigid localities, as well as the tropical islands of the Florida Keys; but it's in the backlands of the old middle South where he has achieved his greatest fame and popularity. This is largely due to the peculiar imagination and interest with which the old-school negro has looked upon this wild creature of the woods and bottom-lands. To them old ring-tail is "brother 'coon"—with hardly a greater difference from his own race as he himself differs from the whites. And the person who has not spent a moonlight fall night huntin' 'coons with a picturesque old Southern negro and one or more good hounds, just ain't completed their hunting or trapping experiences.

The number of 'coons taken by trappers is apt to be a surprise to many who are not familiar with the fur trade. The official report for the 1945-46 season gives an indication of the numbers as well as the distribution of these animals. It must also be remembered that these figures are far from complete, as in no instance do they include these animals that were taken by hunting or otherwise not officially reported. Here are the statistics for some of the top States which compile such reports: Louisiana, 244,502; Texas, 164,327; Michigan, 88,700; Ohio, 56,971; Indiana, 42,400; Iowa, 41,084; Florida, 20,692 (69,524 in 1939); North Carolina, 20,-000 (110,000 in 1941). In Canada the report for 1944 was: Ontario, 21,866; Quebec, 3,651; New Brunswick, 2,180.

When raccoons are born they are blind and helpless, and remain under the care and protection of their parents for the first season at least. Their crying when separated from the old ones somewhat resembles the sound of a human infant under similar circumstances.

The adults also have a sort of whimpering cry which is occasionally heard on moonlight nights, and which varies from the quavering call of a screech owl to the laughing hoot of a big barred owl.

They prefer to make their homes in wooded sections where

there are hollow trees and hollow logs in which to make their dens, and in the vicinity of streams or lakes where they can wander in search of food and sometimes wash their food before eating it. Even the shell-fish, frogs and the like which they catch, are very often carefully washed in the water in which caught. They have even been known to carry other types of food a considerable distance to wash it, before eating.

The raccoon is omnivorous in its feeding habits. In other words, he will eat most anything—meat or vegetables. His diet includes shell-fish, frogs, fish, small animals, birds, eggs, reptiles, insects, corn, nuts, fruit and poultry.

In the colder parts of their range, severe winter weather will generally drive them into a state of semi-hibernation. Young and old will retire to their den in a big hollow tree or elsewhere and they will all curl up together. Sometimes several families will occupy the same hollow tree. If the cold spell is particularly severe and long, the 'coons will lapse into a lethargic state. They may stay in this deep sleep for several days or considerably longer; but their unconsciousness is not so deep that a moderation of the temperature will not send them out in the snow. Back into their dens they will go again, however, if the temperature takes another nosedive. Winter or summer, they are inclined to travel at night; and they seem to be especially equipped with night vision; although they occasionally can be seen wandering around in the bright sunlight.

In addition to the many other items on their menu, the 'coon is very fond of corn, whether it is soft or hard. A corn field at the edge of a big woods is always a good place to look for signs, particularly if it is in a river bottom and not far from a creek or river. They are also fond of honey, grapes, persimmons, palmetto berries, nuts and fresh meat. In fact, they will eat most anything a man will eat—and they are about as particular regarding its freshness and cleanliness.

Raccoons will invariably stop to investigate any shining object in the water. They habitually wade the riffles of streams searching for mussels and other food, and perhaps this fact accounts for their curiosity. Trappers often successfully take advantage of this habit, by attaching a piece of tin foil or a large bright button to the trap pan and setting the trap in shallow, swift water near the bank. When the set is made in the water, it is never necessary to conceal it from view. A properly located cubby set, however, will take more 'coons than any other method. The best place to locate a cubby set is at the junction of small streams, at places where springs flow into a stream, or at any suitable place along a waterway where raccoon signs are found. The best baits are sardines, dried herring, canned salmon or any kind of fish bait. A few white chicken or duck feathers scattered in the rear of the cubby will aid by attracting the 'coons attention.

When tracks of the animals are found along the bank of a stream, and tracking is possible, follow them carefully until the trail leads between two stones or any narrow passageway between or under drift debris, then set your trap in this narrowed path where the animal will be forced to step on it on his next habitual trip along this route. Cover the trap over very lightly with fine grass, light leaves or pulverized soil. Such sets as this are easily made when there is a light snow on the ground.

In trapping raccoons the No. 1½ or No. 2 double-jawed trap should be used, to prevent the crippling and loss of animals that may attempt to chew off the foot underneath the jaws of the trap. They also struggle considerably when in a trap, and it should be well fastened. If a stake is used, it should be a hard dry wood or the 'coon will soon chew it off.

The raccoon likes to potter around in the water, looking for things to eat and making something of a ceremony in washing the things he eats, but he also likes to cross streams over trees or logs that lie across them. In good raccoon country these are always good places to set traps. Chop out a place on top of the log which will hold the trap and cover it with rotten wood or leaves. A few drops of honey or some light colored chicken feathers scattered on the ends of the log will help.

If there is a nice bank along the stream where you are trapping, find a spot where the water is shallow at the base and dig a hole into the bank about a foot or so wide and about two feet wide and three feet deep. Slope the bottom so that the back is dry but the entrance is about two inches under water. Place your trap in the water at the entrance and bait the bank cubby with fresh fish, corn, persimmons, honey or whatever is the natural bait for your particular district. A little scent will help and that made from muskrat glands is good for 'coons.

If you are trapping on your own farm and have a good field of corn, an unhusked bundle or two may pay you a premium. Trapping in even a fairly small field of corn is pretty much of a gamble, but if you will carry a bundle or two well into the woods or up a stream into the 'coon's own territory, there isn't so much competition in the matter of food supply and the animals are pretty sure to go to it. The stream set is the best. Thrust a pole through the bundle and place it in the edge of the water where the top can be leaned against the bank or a tree, with a narrow passageway between the base of the bundle and the obstruction on the shore. One trap should be placed underwater in this passageway. Other traps can be placed around the edge. If the water is too deep on the off-side, build up a platform of sand or mud so the trap will not be too far under the surface. A similar set can be made on dry land in the woods, by leaning the bundle against a large tree. There must, of course, be some unhusked ears of corn on the stalks.

Trail sets are also good. These can generally be found leading from the trees where the 'coons have their dens, or where they travel through marshy ground, into corn fields, through the palmettos and elsewhere. These trails are generally used regularly in their trips to favorite feeding grounds and can be identified by the tracks left in soft spots along them. When you have found such a trail, find a place where it narrows sufficiently to make a set, where it passes close to a tree, stumps, large rock, etc. Dig out enough earth so the pan of the trap will be flush with the ground and cover thinly with grass cuttings or other natural camouflage. To avoid catching domestic stock, deer or other wild creatures much larger than raccoons, cut a small tree and place it across the trail, leaving plenty of room for your prospective game to pass underneath but causing the others to go around.

Raccoon pelts should be stretched open and in a square shape. In skinning, cut straight up the belly from vent to chin and down the inside of all the legs. The square shape is accomplished by the manner in which it is tacked out for drying and not by any additional cutting. The tail should be split and tacked out. Nails should be placed close together to produce an even form when dry. Raccoon pelts are inclined to be unusually fatty, and because of this the skins should be carefully "fleshed" before stretching to dry. A dull knife or hard axe is a good tool for this. If the fat is not properly removed, the fur is apt to slip or the entire pelt becomes oil-burned if not tanned within reasonable time.

The raccoon is one of the cleanest of all wild animals and the flesh is widely used for table purposes.

If you are interested in cultivating the crop of raccoons which happen to be living on your property, do not destroy the big trees where they have their dens! This will only drive them to your neighbor's woods, where he can trap them and pocket the price of the pelts that might have been yours. If they have a sufficiency of natural food, these animals will rarely destroy poultry, and the small amount of corn they eat is more than balanced by the pests which they destroy for your benefit. By protecting their natural food supply, you reduce the risk of loss of your farm produce.

CHAPTER X

THE OPOSSUM

THE opossum is the only animal in North America which belongs to that strange and very ancient order among the animals of the earth whose young are born at an undeveloped stage
and the mother is obliged to carry them about for several weeks
in a kangeroo-like pouch in the skin of her own body. Scientifically this class of creatures are known as "marsupials" or "pouch
animals," and they are placed at the end of the list in the rating
of their intelligent development. They differ from all other animals in many respects. Before they are born the blood of the
mother does *not* circulate through the veins of the unborn, as in
other animals. As a result, at the time of birth, the young mar-
supial is a tiny creature, blind, hairless and almost as helpless as
a little lump of jelly. As they come into the world, the mother
takes them carefully in her front paws and places them in the
hairless pouch or pocket in the skin of her abdomen. The half-
formed tiny creatures have a mouth that is specially formed for
suction, which attaches to one of the nursing teats inside the
pouch; and there they remain attached through the many days
or even weeks while they develop. At length their hair develops
and their eyes open, and they eventually gain enough strength to
stick their little heads outside the pouch and get their first look
at the strange world. Even after they come to the stage where they

can venture outside, they will scurry back inside again at the first sign of danger. Opossums are very prolific, having from five to fourteen young at a litter; and in some cases more than one litter a year.

Although with a limited importance as a fur bearer and so easy to trap that it requires only elementary information and skill, the opossum cannot be ignored in any anthology of trapping.

There are three scientifically recognized varieties of opossums (*Didelphis virginiana*):

The Virginia Opossum (*Didelphis virginiana virginiana*), which is the principal variety, ranges from the Hudson Valley westward to the Great Lakes and south almost to the Gulf of Mexico in Texas. Strictly speaking, however, this animal is a "product of the South." About the size of a house cat, it has a long head, with slender muzzle; its long tail, pink ears and the bottoms of its feet are naked. It is a very hairy animal, the under-fur being wooly and white, while the outer coat is straight, coarse and tipped with black. The eyes are like a pair of shiny black shoe-buttons. Its tail is used like that of a monkey's, by which it can hang head-down from the limb of a tree with apparent comfort.

The Florida Opossum (*Didelphis virginiana pigra*) is found in Florida, the lower coast region of Georgia and westward through the low Gulf Coast regions to western Louisiana. It is somewhat smaller than the Virginia variety, but to all other outward appearances very much the same.

The Texas Opossum (*Didelphis mesamericana texensis*) is found along the coastal regions of Texas and the Lower Rio Grande Valley. This is a large opossum and it appears in two separate color phases: a gray phase quite similar to Virginia, and a black phase in which the long guard hairs are black and the rear half black.

In spite of the comparatively limited area over which the opossum makes its home, there were thirteen States which reported a catch of more than 50,000 pelts officially taken by trappers during the 1945-46 season. This does not include the many thousands that were taken by hunters and trappers who did not report them. Virginia leads the list with 330,066; Missouri next

OPOSSUM

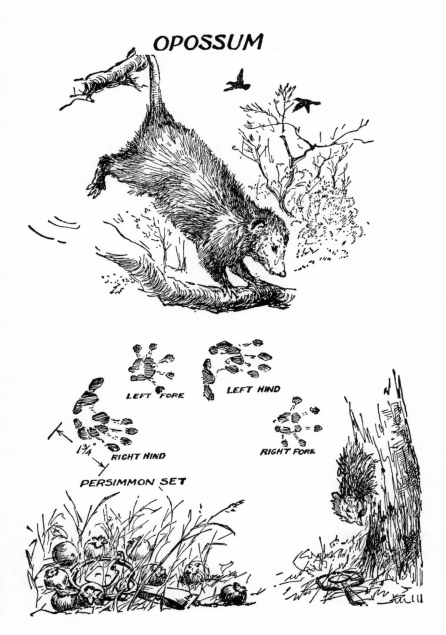

LEFT FORE LEFT HIND

RIGHT HIND RIGHT FORE

1¾"

PERSIMMON SET

with 261,359 (it was 463,119 for 1941); Oklahoma, 185,001;
Arkansas, 122,593 (430,980 in 1942); Kansas, 98,645; etc.

Incidentally, there does not seem to be any general decrease in
the numbers of opossum trapped during the past several years;
and, more important, the animal seem to be extending their range
gradually northward.

The opossum is omnivorous—which means that it will eat most
anything that can be chewed. Its menu ranges through a long
list of wild fruit, berries, fish, eggs, insects, young birds and animals, soft-shelled nuts, frogs, green corn, roots, etc. It forages on
the ground and in the tree tops. It prefers a wooded area for its
home, usually burrowing under the roots of a large tree, where it
is difficult for a hunter to dig it out; although sometimes a
hollow log is chosen for such housekeeping as a family of opossums indulge. Like the bear and woodchuck, it stores up under its
own skin an extra supply of fat for winter, when food is scarce
and dear; but living as it does in the South, the frigidity of a long
white winter is not generally one of its major worries. And above
all, the mother's nice warm baby pouch in the skin of her belly,
relieves her of the responsibility of leaving the little ones in any
nest to catch their death of cold or be eaten by some enemy. And
speaking of eating is a reminder that a not-too-fat opossum is a
pretty tasty dish for any man's dinner table. Served roasted properly browned, with sweet potatoes, yellow corn-bread and strong
coffee, it leaves but little to be desired. But half the enjoyment of
a feast on opossum is to have captured them yourself on the moonlight hunt in the wooded hills of their native haunts.

One of this animal's peculiar habits, which has become an
American proverb, is its deliberate "playing 'possum." When
captured it will invariably pretend death, thus apparently having
the idea that it will be left without being further disturbed.

Most people believe that this "playing 'possum" is just an act.
But scientists have by careful observation about decided that this
seemingly lifeless condition is something more than mere pretense,
and is really brought about by a nervous shock somewhat similar
to fainting spells of human beings.

All in all, the opossum is a dull-witted, slow-moving creature,
so ill-fitted by Nature to protect itself by manly defense or speedy

retreat, that it might almost be considered defenseless. Even as a pet it shows off very poorly and is highly uninteresting. In the daytime, as a captive or in its own wild native haunts, its sole desire is to curl up into a furry ball and sleep. If disturbed, it merely opens its pink mouth very widely in a sort of rather ferocious silent yawn; but as soon as the trouble is over, back to sleep it goes. All of which is not very exciting, but highly interesting to all those who love the out-doors and the wild creatures who dwell in it.

The Negroes of the Southern States have a feeling that ol' 'possum was created especially for their special benefit and delight. They say, and perhaps with more truth than testimony, that "no white man can ever fully appreciate the delicious joy of a moon-light 'possum hunt or the real delicate flavor of a roasted 'possum." When a couple of old darkie cronies get together with their cur dogs and go out into the wooded hills to hunt 'possum in the moonlight, life for them is really worth while. And coming back to the humblest shack on Tobacco Road, with two or more live 'possums suspended with their tails securely wedged between a split sapling stick, is for these the culmination of a night well spent. Then they are generally fattened for a couple of weeks for the feast.

The opossum is easily trapped. The No. 1 or No. 1½ trap will take him. The set can be made in most any natural recess in the base of an old tree; a hollow log, crevice in a rocky ledge, under the roots of a tree or a constructed cubby are all good places. There are only two very important things—that there are 'pos-sums in the vicinity and to have some high-smelling bait to attract their attention. Any tainted old meat, chicken heads etc., and it is best to fasten it down in the back part of your set. Then place the trap in the entrance and cover lightly with grass, leaves or whatever is the natural material for camouflage.

The hollow log set is also good for 'possum, using a high-smell-ing bait, of course. They can even be taken by just nailing the bait to the side of a tree so that it hangs a foot or so from the ground and placing the trap directly underneath. Bait sets made in orchards near thickly wooded areas are desirable; as well as under a persimmon tree. In the latter instance, just gather together a considerable number of the ripe fruit and arrange them around your trap after it has been set and covered with a little grass or other camouflage.

Sprinkling a little scent lure around your set will do no harm and it may add to your catch. Fish oil makes a desirable lure for opossum, although some trappers merely use rancid lard. In any instance, the stronger the smell the more opossums you are apt to catch.

Opossums should be case skinned and stretched flesh side out. Cut off the tail and legs; and remove surplus fat.

CHAPTER XI

THE OTTER

THE otter is in many respects the most interesting of all North American fur-bearing animals; and although it is found from Alaska to Florida and from Labrador to California, it is by far the scarcest pelt procured by trappers in most of the States where it is found. The otter is one of the best present day examples of an animal that is in the process of transition from living on the land to living almost entirely in the water. Because of his extreme fondness for fish he has followed the life of a fisherman so long and so intensively that he has almost lost his ability to make a living anywhere but in the water, and he has even grown to look and act very much like a seal. His cousins, the sea otter, have become almost completely "marine," but with the land otter the transition is still taking place. Except for man, it has practically no enemies, because of its very remarkable skill as a fast and elusive swimmer.

There are nine scientifically recognized varieties of Otter (*Lutra canadensis* and related forms) in North America.

The Canada Otter (*Lutra canadensis canadensis*) is found over a large area from north of the Arctic Circle in Alaska, Yukon and Northwest Territories southeasterly across Canada to Labrador and the northeastern part of the United States as far south as the coast of South Carolina. It is, however, scattered spottily over this wide area and nowhere can it be called plentiful. Its pelage is uniformly a rich, glossy, dark brown; grayish on the cheeks; belly somewhat lighter, with a grayish tinge; and the short under-fur is thick and particularly soft and fine. The sexes are colored alike and but little difference in size. The total average length ranges from 40 to 45 inches, with a tail vertebrae from 12 to 15 inches; and the weight generally ranges from 18 to 25 pounds.

The Newfoundland Otter (*Lutra degener*) is found only on the island of Newfoundland. This is the smallest of the otters, with a comparatively long tail and the pelt is particularly dark on the back and lighter on sides of the head and neck.

The Carolina Otter (*Lutra canadensis lataxina*) is found in North and South Carolina. It is medium in size and lighter in color than the previously described varieties. The sides of the head and neck are generally a pale yellowish and the soles of the feet are less hairy.

The Florida Otter (*Lutra canadensis vaga*) ranges through Florida and eastern Georgia. This variety is somewhat larger than the previously described otters, with a longer tail and is reddish in color.

The Interior Otter (*Lutra canadensis interior*) is found in Nebraska and adjacent mid-west States. It is the largest of all the otters; dark reddish brown in color.

The California Otter (*Lutra canadensis brevipilosus*) is found in California, principally through the valleys and drainages of the Sacramento and San Joaquin rivers. In general the pelage is some-what shorter than in other varieties and the coloration pale, with light-tipped guard hairs and light brown on throat.

The Sonora Otter (*Lutra canadensis sonora*) is found in Arizona and southern California. It is large in size; and in color-ation pale brown on back and light grayish brown on underparts, with sides of head and neck pale yellowish or even cream colored.

The Pacific Otter (*Lutra canadensis pacifica*) ranges over a rather large area through the Pacific Northwest from Oregon to the coastal regions of Alaska. This is a large otter, comparatively dark on the back, with the underparts much lighter.

The Queen Charlotte or Island Otter (*Lutra periclyzomae*) is found only on the Queen Charlotte Islands, British Columbia. This variety is now apparently extinct.

OTTER

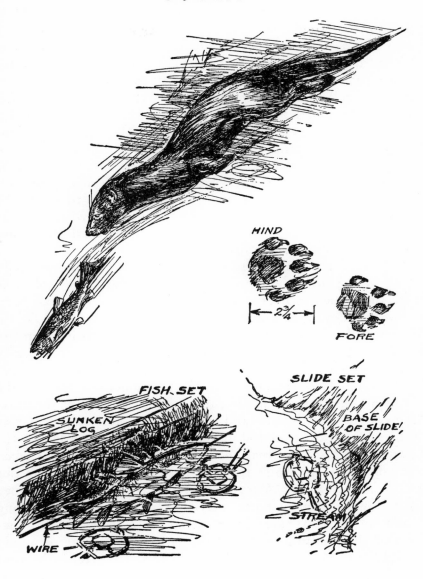

HIND

FORE

2¾

FISH SET

SUNKEN LOG

WIRE

SLIDE SET

BASE OF SLIDE

STREAM

A very convincing evidence of the general scarcity of otters in the United States today is given by the last report of the U. S. Government Fish and Wild Life Service. For the entire trapping season of 1945-'46 a total of only 6,571 of these animals were officially tabulated as having been taken. The latest report for Canada was 12,089. That is a pretty small total. In the U. S. there were only 9 States that reported more than 100 otters being trapped. The four leading States were: Louisiana, 2,367; Alaska, 1,721; Virginia, 555; Washington, 401. The top figures for Canada were: Ontario, 4,411; Quebec, 3,970; and Manitoba, 1,952. So far as the U. S. is concerned, these animals should be protected by law—and the trappers should be the first to petition the Brass Hats in the State and National capitals to enact the necessary legal measures for this protection. Otherwise, this fine fur bearer is apt to pass into that oblivion of total extinction from which there is no earthly return.

The otter is not nearly as prolific as most other fur bearers, only 1 to 3 young being born to a litter. Throughout most of their range they breed in February or March and the young are born in April or May. It is usually somewhat earlier in the deep South. The home den is generally at the end of burrow with an under-water entrance in stream or lake—although they occasionally make their nest in a cave or at the bottom of a hollow tree. Sometimes there is more than one exit, the additional one being at the end of another burrow leading in an entirely different direction for a considerable distance and coming to an end under-water or to the surface of the ground in some well-hidden spot. It is in the darkness of these dens that the baby otters are born; and when first taken into the water they are not only unable to swim but show a noticeable fear of trying to. But it is not long before they are following their parents, particularly the mother, on long swimming trips. Apparently the otters mate for the entire duration of their natural lives, and the father is far more of an aid to rearing the youngsters than in most cases. The otter is the most expert swimmer of all the fur bearers. In fact, there are few creatures who are capable of excelling them. One of the choice sights in the wilds is to witness a mother otter and her offspring having-a-time for themselves in some deep slow-moving river or

a lake. It is quite obvious that they enjoy life, as well as each
other's companionship. When little Mary or Willie Otter gets
tired he just climbs on Mamma's back and rides. When she dives,
the youngsters follow and their heads generally pop up above the
surface at the same instant. A mother otter will protect her young
ones to the extent of sacrificing her own life in so doing. The
average dog that makes the mistake of tangling with an otter will
be lucky if he gets out of the battle in condition to go home with
his master.

Otters are so expert at swimming that they can catch any fish
that swims, by fairly swimming them down in spite of all their
fast twisting and darting; and where fish are reasonably plentiful
an otter can in this manner easily catch ten times as many fish as
he can eat. They are also excellent judges of the different kinds of
fish, according to human tastes, generally preferring trout, salmon, eels and small fish.

The family life of these animals is in many respects more
strongly bonded than with most other animals. Mother, father
and youngster keep together, in most instances, until the young
otters find mates of their own and set up housekeeping for themselves. They are great travelers, and the whole family goes along
on these fishing expeditions which sometimes takes them on a two-
to three-week excursion over a good many miles of river and small
stream. They will follow the course of a small stream until the
water practically gives out; then they will take off overland to
the headwater of some other stream. On these trips they generally
travel single file and always pick the easiest way around all obstructions, and follow the same trail each time they make the trip.
Nor do they spend all of the time at fishing, often taking time out
to romp and play like happy puppies when they come to nice
grassy places on the bank or among the trees. During these playful
romps they also do considerable digging and clawing up the soft
turf—which the keen trapper can easily identify by examination.
But they seem to get the greatest fun out of sliding-down-hill,
where the bank is sufficiently steep and smooth enough to make a
nice toboggan into the water. These places are easily identified.
And they generally have a path leading up to the top again. A
family of otters will spend an hour or more at a time sliding down

one of these chutes, time after time, just like boys sliding down a snow-covered hill on their sleds.

The best place to find otters in midwinter when the streams are frozen and the snow is deep, is around swift rapids or where the water is otherwise kept open. And even in winter they indulge in their favorite sport of sliding-down-hill on the snow.

In trapping otter it is well to remember that they come to a bait quite readily, although they are smart, shy and exceptionally strong. Nothing smaller than a No. 3, or even a No. 4 trap should be used; and it takes a well placed trap to catch them, and, if a drowning set cannot be rigged, it takes a strongly fastened chain to hold them. Fish is good bait and fish oil, muskrat musk or beaver castor can be added to good effect.

A good place to make a whole fish set is beside a sunken log in about eighteen inches of water. Run a wire through the entire length of the fish and fasten it on the bottom alongside the log in as natural a position as possible. It is best to use two traps and place them on the bottom a few inches opposite the head and tail of the fish; and anchor them securely to a heavy rock or iron weight so that the otter when caught will drown.

Another good set is along one of the small tributary streams where the animals travel. Remembering that the otter does not like to climb over things, a few good size logs laid across a narrow part of his course, with an opening or gateway at a suitable place to set the trap or traps will do the trick. If logs are not available, stick branches in the ground or pile limbs to form the obstruction. As otters generally travel in pairs or families, it is sometimes smart to leave two openings and make two sets. You may get an otter in each set.

If you find a well-used slide, this too is generally good for one or more catches. Traps should be set at the bottom of the slide, in 8 to 12 inches of water—and a sliding wire run out into deep water for drowning. Other traps can be set at the base of the trails where they crawl out to climb to the top of the slide. This latter trap should be set close to the bank, in only two or three inches of water.

Some otters are taken in cubbies. If you can find a natural crevice in the bank close to the water level, it is better than to dig out a hole for the set. It is a good idea to dig suitable cubbies long before the trapping season opens, if suitable natural ones are not available. Bait can be whole fish, a frog or crawfish; and it can be fastened right to the pan of the trap, just above the water, inside the cubby.

If you find a large log with one end submerged in the water, set a trap just under the surface of the water and scatter some beaver castor or muskrat scent on the log just above it.

The otter is always case-skinned and stretched flesh side out; with the tail split to the end and stretched flat. The skin can be reversed, after fully dry. The skin of these animals is not only hard to remove, but difficult to flesh.

CHAPTER XII

THE WILD CAT

THE "cat" family is far less extensively and less spectacularly represented among the wild animals in North America than it is in most of the other continents of the earth. We have but two general classifications of creatures which in any way are comparable to the lion, leopard, tiger or other big cats of Africa, Asia and even South America. Our representatives are the mountain lion or cougar and the wild cat—the latter of which is the only important fur bearer.

In speaking of the wild cat family, it naturally includes the lynx, which is little more than a long-haired variety of what is commonly referred to as the bobcat or bay lynx. To the naturalists the Bobcat (*Lynx rufus rufus* and related forms) is represented by ten different varieties and the Lynx (*Lynx canadensis canadensis* and related forms) has three representatives. These are the only two scientifically recognized classifications of the wild cat family which can broadly be claimed for North America; and between them they range over the continent from Point Barrow, at the Arctic northernmost tip of Alaska, to the tropical Everglades of Florida, and from Newfoundland to the desert regions of Arizona and the southernmost California.

The true Bobcat (*Lynx rufus rufus*) is found over a considerable part of the eastern half of the United States from Maine to

North Dakota and as far south as Georgia. He is very much like a much overgrown house-cat with unusually long heavy legs, prominent ears, very short tail and particularly big feet. The pelage is a variable brownish mixed with buff or reddish and with somewhat indistinctly lined brown spots, darkest along the back; legs lighter; crown of head inclined to be streaked with dark brown or black; outside of ears black, sometimes with gray spots; small black tuft on ear; tip and back of tail black, and belly whitish. They are paler all over in winter than summer. Total length about 36 inches and average weight up to 20 to 25 pounds.

The Nova Scotia Bobcat (*Lynx gigas*) is found only in that Canadian province. This is one of the largest of all the bobcats, powerfully built and with a large head. In coloration it is richer and darker than most varieties, with considerable black on the underparts.

The Florida Bobcat (*Lynx rufus floridanus*) ranges through Florida, north into central Georgia and west into Louisiana. It is somewhat smaller than the Nova Scotia although larger than the type Bobcat—averaging around 38 to 40 inches in total length for a big male. It is, however, more slender in proportion to its height and length, with much smaller feet. In coloration it is darker than either of the preceding, with more black and less of the reddish brown tinge, which gives the typical *rufus* its name.

The Bailey or Plateau Bobcat (*Lynx baileyi*) is found in Arizona, New Mexico, western Texas, southern Colorado and southeastern California. It is considerably smaller than any of the preceding; and its pelage predominates in soft grays and buffy browns, with one blackish and one brownish band in front of black tip on tail. The pelage is even grayer in winter.

The Mountain Bobcat (*Lynx uinta*) is found in the mountainous regions of New Mexico, Utah, Colorado and Wyoming. This is the largest of the bobcats, large males attaining a length of 42 inches. It has large hind feet and a comparatively long tail with two black bands on top in front of the black tip. The pelage on the back is a mixture of buffy, gray and black, without the more distinct darker spots; belly whitish, spotted with dark or even black; yellowish brown on throat.

The Desert Bobcat (*Lynx rufus eremicus*) ranges through the desert regions of Arizona and eastern California. It is medium in size. In color it is pale yellowish brown tinged with gray or black on back, lightly spotted or striped with brown or blackish; belly whitish; and 6 or 7 black stripes on tail.

The Texas Bobcat (*Lynx rufus texensis*) ranges in southern and eastern Texas. It is heavily spotted on both back and belly, and a rich rufus in coloration.

The California Bobcat (*Lynx rufus californicus*) is found through most of California west of the desert regions. This is one of the smallest of all the bobcats. Its pelage is reddish brown mixed with gray and blackish, darker along the back; and has a broad collar of rusty gray spotted with black.

The Barred Bobcat (*Lynx fasciatus fasciatus*) is found in the northwestern coastal regions of California, along the entire coast of Oregon, Washington and southern British Columbia. It is a rich chestnut-brown with sprinkling of black on back; legs barred with dark brown or even black; belly white, strongly spotted with black; terminal third to half of tail black.

The Pallid Barred Bobcat (*Lynx fasciatus pallescens*) is found in northern interior California, across northern Nevada and Utah into Colorado, the range extending northward through eastern Oregon and Washington and eastward through Idaho into Wyoming. This is a very small bobcat, attaining a maximum total length of only 30 to 32 inches. The Pallid Barred Bobcat is also particularly light in color, especially on the head and face; with black on ears.

The Canada Lynx (*Lynx canadensis canadensis*) ranges over a wide area from Pennsylvania westward intermittently to Colorado and the Pacific coast of Oregon, northward through Canada to the edge of the Barren Lands. It is somewhat larger than the largest of the bobcats, also heavier in build and with longer pelage, larger feet, prominent ruff about throat and very prominent tufts at tip of ears. The pelage is pale gray at the base near the skin, then buffy brown and tipped with a mixture of gray, dark brown and black. The cheeks and nose are gray; top of head brownish; inside of ears are grayish, edged with buff, a gray spot on the outside surface of each; tail brownish with black tip; and underparts lighter. There are irregular blotches of blackish, most notice-

BOBCAT and LYNX

LYNX

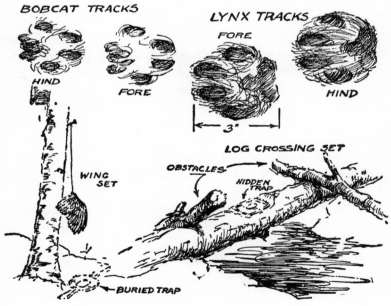

BOBCAT TRACKS

HIND

FORE

LYNX TRACKS

FORE

HIND

3"

WING SET

LOG CROSSING SET

OBSTACLES

HIDDEN TRAP

BURIED TRAP

able on the belly. In summer the coloration is somewhat browner than in winter.

The Arctic Lynx (*Lynx canadensis mallipilosus*) is found in northwestern North America from Point Barrow south into British Columbia. This is the largest of all our wild cats, attaining a length of 42 inches or even more. It is inclined to be browner, with less gray, than the Canada Lynx, and with particularly dense, soft, wooly fur. Its tail is comparatively long and the feet unusually large—the hind feet sometimes being as much as 11 inches.

The Newfoundland Lynx (*Lynx subsolanus*) is found only on that island. It resembles the Canada Lynx in size and general coloration, although somewhat darker and richer in tone.

The Indian called the Bobcat "Pishpish" or "Kivalas." The Alaskan Eskimo calls the Lynx "Nituyak," and the Mackenzie Eskimo calls it "Pitaksikok."

Both the bobcat and the lynx have many habits in common, although one is a dweller in warm or even arid desert regions, while the other has chosen a range which is cold to Arctic. The lynx is more of a forest creature, preferring deep woods, while some of the bobcats make their homes in the big forested swamps of the south. Neither hibernate, and the broad furred feet of the lynx serve him as snowshoes in traveling over the soft snow of the northern winter. They are both exceedingly wary and difficult to observe. They are normally nocturnal in their habits, particularly in regions frequented by human beings, although they occasionally move about during the day in the wilder regions. The bobcat is the less furtive of the two and sometimes makes its home in fairly thickly settled areas.

A few figures on the number of wild cat that were recently taken by trappers gives an idea of the present plentifulness of these animals. Of the two classifications, the lynx is of course the most important from the standpoint of the fur trade; which means that we should scan the Alaskan and Canadian records. During 1945 there were only 922 lynx taken in Alaska, as compared to 2,705 for 1939. During the 1943-'44 season there were 10,191 lynx taken in Canada, as compared to 6,684 for 1940-'41. In the U. S. during the 1945-'46 season there were only 480 lynx officially reported as taken—384 in Wisconsin and 96 in North Dakota. British Columbia leads all districts with 2,625; Quebec, 1,819; Northwest Territories, 1,803.

The bobcat catch shows a little more satisfactory picture. For the last officially recorded catch the U. S. total was 21,140. New Mexico leads with 5,276; Minnesota reported 3,085; Michigan, 2,910; California, 2,063; and Texas, Colorado, Washington and Mississippi all with well over 1,000.

The lynx, incidentally, is also found in the northern parts of both Asia and Europe. In ancient times the Europeans had many peculiar beliefs associated with this supposedly mysterious creature. One of these beliefs was that it possessed the power of seeing through any and all substances from the log wall of a building to a full-sized mountain. Hence we have the expression "lynx-eyed," which is even today sometimes used in describing persons who seem to be able to see with unusual vision.

The lynx of the northern woods is a most interesting creature. Those who know him well are apt to think of him as something of a ghost-like creature, merely because of his uncanny ability to travel through the woods in either summer or winter with such stealth and quiet ease. His snow-shoe-like paws are capable of supporting him on soft snow or dry leaves with practically no noise at all; and his long sinewy legs can carry him in long, silent leaps, almost as though he had wings. Even his color is such that he is about the most difficult of all animals to see in his natural background, whether it is woods, brush or open snow. He is a good tree climber and also a good swimmer. To the rabbits of every district where lynx are to be found, this tufted-eared, jowl-whiskered, long-legged wild cat is undoubtedly the embodiment of the worst fears they know. He is in truth a fearsome appearing beast, particularly when caught in a trap; however, as every trapper who has had much experience with him knows, he is at heart quite a bluffer and a coward.

The lynx is particularly notorious for its occasional calls, which are much like the magnified noises of a domestic cat. They mew, yowl, cater-waul, hiss, spit and growl. When heard in the deep woods on a winter night, it is something to remember. These calls of the lynx are often mistaken for that of a mountain lion.

They both have from one to four young to a litter, which are born from March to June, depending upon the latitude of their home.

The lynx is more desirable than the southern bobcat, as a fur bearer; but from a predatory control standpoint, they should both be trapped.

Trapping has been found to be one of the most effective methods of bobcat and lynx control. On its wild range these animals feed to a large extent upon rabbits and other rodents, but they also prey upon such valuable forms of wildlife as antelope, deer, and other game animals, especially the fawns, and ground-nesting birds. With human occupation of its former haunts, it finds the young of domestic livestock very satisfactory substitutes for its ordinary fare in the wild. When its food is less easily obtained in nature than among the flocks and herds of the range country, they may become exceedingly destructive to domestic livestock, especially to sheep during the lambing season, to pigs, goats, and calves, and to poultry. The depredations of bobcats in parts of Arkansas in recent years have made hog raising on an extensive scale impracticable in some localities. Losses caused by this predatory animal among sheep are particularly severe when lambing is conducted on the open range and the lambing grounds are in close proximity to the broken, rough, rocky canyons that favor the presence of the bobcat. Sheepmen often choose such rugged country grounds for lambing because of the protection it affords against storms.

On gaining entry into a flock of sheep at lambing time, commonly under cover of darkness, the bobcat carries on its depredations in such manner as to cause little commotion there. The lamb is usually killed by a characteristic bite on the back of the neck or head, and then it is pulled down to be eaten. If its lust for killing is not satisfied, the bobcat may kill other lambs by the same method, continuing its work quietly until a large number have been destroyed.

The bobcat is less fearsome than the lynx, but at heart he is the same sort of critter. They were once quite common in most all of the thickly wooded sections of the United States, but are now restricted to the most thinly settled backwoods districts, and nowhere are they plentiful. Hillsides and clearings overgrown with brush and brambles and young growth are quite as much to their liking as dense forests.

They generally hunt alone and resort to quick dashes at fast speed to overtake their game, rather than the perseverant and tireless stalking which makes foxes, weasels and other hunters so proficient. They are still-hunters, after the manner of most of the cat tribe. When a bobcat, or lynx, hears the faintest sound in the underbrush, he quickly and silently maneuvers into position, slinking and crouching ready to spring, until the unsuspecting victim is within range of a flashing dash and quick capture. Sometimes, when hunting, he utters a wild scream from time to time; apparently for the purpose of so startling any creature nearby that it will dash from its hiding place. The wildcat's sense of smell is not good, but they have good eyesight and wonderful hearing.

Both the bobcat and the lynx do most of their traveling in the twilight of evening and morning, although they are frequently seen in midday in sections where human beings are few and far between. They like to sleep in hollow trees, caverns among the rocks, under a tent-like spruce tree or a dense thicket. They also like to lie on a big windfall, the branch of a large tree or a rocky point in the sun.

Bobcats are easily caught in traps of the common double-spring steel type, in sizes 2 and 3, or the No. 2 Coil Spring Fox Trap is an excellent wildcat trap.

In selecting a site for trap sets, one should be guided to a large extent by the tracks of the animals and by other traces of its presence, which are commonly found in the rugged recesses of the open range. Such places as leached limestone ridges, limestone cap rock, or eroded granitic canyons containing an abundance of small caverns and holes surrounded by rather extensive underbrush form the ideal habitat of the bobcat. This may be in low-lying country or in adjacent higher mountainous areas.

Though it is advisable to use the greatest caution in setting bobcat and lynx traps, the care with which the art is practiced need not be so great as in the case of the wolf or the coyote.

When the trail of the bobcat has been found along or leading from its rocky lair, traps may be placed in either double or single sets. If the trail is not frequently used by livestock also, or by such big-game animals as deer, the so-called "blind" trap set may be employed. This set is called a blind because no lure or scent need be used around it when completed.

Whether single or double blind trap sets are employed, they should be placed in holes dug directly in the trail of the bobcat close to such an obstruction as an exposed root, a rock, or a clump of weeds; for the bobcat seldom fails to step over rather than on such an obstruction in its path. If the double set is to be used, the trap holes should be only about 1 inch apart, separated just far enough to prevent interference of the jaws when the trap is sprung. Each hole should be dug only slightly larger than the size of the trap and just deep enough to hold the set trap and allow this to be slightly lower than the level of the surrounding ground. When two traps are used, they may be joined together with a lap link at the ends of their chains, which in turn may be attached to a stake pin driven slightly below the ground level, or a drag may be used either made of wrought iron or consisting of a fairly heavy stone. The drag should be bedded under the traps, in which case more excavating will be required. After the trap has been firmly bedded, it is advisable to cover it with fine pulverized earth similar to that found in the mound of a pocket gopher. This will do for the spring of the trap. Dry and finely pulverized horse or cow manure may be more advantageously used to cover the inside of the trap jaws. A trap pad made of canvas or of old descented slicker cloth for finally covering the pan should now be placed on the inside of the jaws; then over all should be sprinkled dry dirt to the depth of a quarter to a half inch, of the same color as the ground surrounding the trap. The spot where the trap is buried should be left in as natural a condition as possible.

A scent, attractive to bobcats, may be used to advantage to lure the animals to trap sets. When scenting is resorted to, however, the traps should not be placed in the runway proper, but on either side of it, or on one side only, and parallel to the trail. They should be set in the same manner as described for the blind sets, between the trail and the spot selected for scattering the scent. This spot should be no more than six to eight inches from the trap. In placing the scent, advantage should be taken of any stubble, bunch of weeds, exposed root, or object used as a scent post.

In passing along its trails, the bobcat will usually revisit these scent posts. When natural scent posts cannot be readily found, one may be easily established along the determined trail by dropping scent on a few clusters of weeds, spears of grass or stubble of low brush. The trap should be set between the trail and the place scented, about six or eight inches from each. Any number of such scent stations may be placed along a determined trail.

The scent used can be the fish oil scent and to this may be added beaver castors, musk glands from mink, weasel, or muskrats. Oil of catnip, diluted in the proportion of 35 drops of the pure oil to 2 ounces of petrolatum, has proved an effective lure in bobcat trapping.

Wild cats can be induced to enter cubby sets if built along their trails. These cubbies should be built of material at hand and made to look natural, narrow at the bottom and high enough so the cat can enter standing up. Place scent in rear of cubby and hang up a rabbit skin, grouse wing, or chicken wing to give him something to look at. Set trap in narrow entrance and place a stone or other object about seven inches in front of trap. This will cause the cat to step over this object into the concealed trap.

One of the best places to look for bobcat signs is around an old log landing or other open place, or around large ant hills. They have a habit of coming regularly to such places to drop their excrement or urine. When such a place is located you can be pretty sure that the same cat or others like him will visit this place within a few days. Survey the place and its surroundings carefully and pick the best spot to make your set. It may be at the base or near to the ant hill, or it may be off to one side. Remember that one catch may be all you will make at the ant hill; but a set made off to one side is not so apt to disturb the location and cause other cats to avoid the place.

While wild cats are good swimmers, they do not particularly like to get their feet wet. In fact, they will generally go a considerable distance to cross even a small stream on a tree or windfall across it; or where they can step from one dry stone to another. If such a place can be found, do some careful figuring on how you can place a trap so that the animal must step into it. This may be at the end of the crossing log or it may be on a moss-covered rock—with the trap, of course, camouflaged to look like the moss covering. Even in such places it is best to use a drag on the trap, so the animal will get away a short distance and not disturb the location.

Both the bobcat and the lynx habitually do their traveling, on hunting trips, in large circles. The abundance of game to their liking generally determines how large a circle and how much territory they will cover. Where food is not plentiful, the complete covering of their hunting route may take as much as two weeks. Or they may make the rounds in two or three days if game is abundant. They are apt to travel farther in winter when snow is on the ground.

Also remember that when they cross the top of a ridge it is invariably at some low place and they will normally cross it at the same spot each time. Such places are generally good places to make baited cubby sets. Scent helps, although their sense of smell is not the best and they will miss it entirely if it is too far from where they pass.

If the area is inclined to be swampy, the cats will make their course to take advantage of walking along the tops of any fallen log that happens to lie in the general direction they want to travel. They like to walk these logs even in thickets. It is generally quite easy to chop out a place in such old logs to set a trap and conceal it with moss or pieces of bark. After the trap is set, place a small branch or other obstacle about six inches on either side of where the trap is hidden so the cat will have to step over it and into the trap.

Some trappers get good results from hanging a rabbit skin or grouse wing on a string over a trap. If it is hung by a string it will rotate or swing with the wind currents and attract the cat's attention to come and investigate.

Oil of catnip, diluted in the proportion of 35 drops of the pure oil to 2 ounces of petrolatum, has proved an effective lure in bobcat trapping. As this is a fine oil, the petrolatum is used to give it body, and this tends also to prevent loss of the scent when exposed to rain. Pure catnip oil is manufactured at a few places in the United States, but if the pure oil is not obtainable, the leaves of the catnip plant may be boiled to a pulpy consistency in water, and this will produce a mild tincture of catnip, which can be drawn off. Catnip in this form has been used as a lure by some trappers with a fair degree of success. A few drops of the mixture of petrolatum and pure catnip oil, or of the tincture, should be placed on the scent spot every third day.

Some Fish and Wildlife Service hunters employ this lure by burying at one side of a bobcat runway a small glass jar or bottle into which has been dropped gauze or cotton batting, saturated with catnip oil. The mouth of the container is left open, but level with the ground, and is protected by a perforated top. If the top is bright, it should be made inconspicuous by moistening it, and while wet brushing it over with dust or sand. Trap sets placed as described around such scent points have accounted for many bobcats.

Both bobcat and lynx should be skinned for drying in a cased fashion and stretched fur side out. The tail should be split, and the feet and claws left on the skin—but be sure to skin out the feet so that all of the bones are removed to the last joint at the base of each of the claws.

CHAPTER XIII

THE FOX

THE fox has the reputation of being the smartest of all our wild animals. As well known in the Old World as in the New, this little fine-furred wild dog has for centuries been the inspiration for an untold number of folk lore tales, story book yarns, cartoons, editorials, jests and philosophical idioms—to say nothing of the hundreds of thousands of fine ladies whose beauty he has enhanced with his decorative pelt. He is to some the best loved and to others the most hated of animals. He has been incessantly hunted afoot, on horseback, with dogs, gun and traps. He is brazenly bold and defiant of all his many enemies and the encroachment of civilization; yet he is not only able to hold his own in the important matter of his own welfare and native population, but thrives and prospers in the face of everything. He will run a pack of well-trained hounds from sunrise to sunset and all night; then lose them with the ease of taking wing like a shooting star. Some experienced fox hunters even say that a wise old red fox really enjoys being chased by a pack of hounds. He's the most interesting, exasperating, destructive, constructive, paradoxical creature on earth.

Of course, not all foxes are the same. As a matter of scientific fact, there is a total of thirty-seven different varieties of foxes in North America and this does not include the several color phases of some of them. There is a great deal of difference between these various foxes, not only in general appearance but also in their habits, personality and intelligence.

There are four principal types of foxes in North America. These are: the Red Fox, Kit Fox or Swift, Gray Fox and Arctic Fox. Taken as a whole, they are found in practically every section of North America, from Point Barrow to Florida and from Greenland to the Rio Grande.

Of the Red Fox there are twelve scientifically recognized varieties. Among these there is considerable similarity in the general color pattern. The sexes are colored alike, although the males are somewhat larger than the females. The predominant coloration is a bright golden yellowish, somewhat darker along the back; the rump is grizzled with whitish, as is also the head; the front feet are black to the elbow and back feet black; the tail has a yellowish tinge, mixed with black and having a black spot on top near the base and a white tip. The animal's belly is generally white. In most, if not all of the varieties of the Red Fox (*Vulpes fulva*), however, there are three color phases: the common "red" phase; the moderately rare "cross" phase; and the rare "black" or "silver" phase. Incidentally, all three of these color phases may occur in the same litter.

The basis for determining separate scientific varieties among animals is sometimes restricted to a peculiar shape of the bones in their head, or their teeth, etc. Such matters are generally of little or no concern to the trapper or even the naturalist in the broader sense. Because of this, the following descriptions only cover such features which are visibly obvious.

The Eastern Red Fox (*Vulpes fulva*) is found throughout northeastern United States. This is the type variety, as above described. The large males average around 41 inches in total length, with a 15 to 16 inch tail vertebrae.

The Nova Scotia Red Fox (*Vulpes rubricosa rubricosa*) is found in Nova Scotia. It is somewhat larger than the above; in coloration it is the darkest of all the red foxes; and has a particularly large bushy tail.

The Newfoundland Red Fox (*Vulpes deletrix*) is found only in Newfoundland. Coloration very pale, light straw yellow; feet not so black; tail light and without black spot at base; and large hind feet. Small in size.

The Labrador Red Fox (*Vulpes rubricosa bangsi*) is found in Labrador. Similar to type except for small ears, and less black on ears and feet.

The Northern Plains Red Fox (*Vulpes regalis*) is found from Minnesota and Manitoba westward through the Dakotas and Alberta. Color a beautiful golden yellow; light face and rear part of back; tail long; black on feet restricted but intense. Males considerably larger than females.

The Long-tailed Red Fox (*Vulpes macroura*) ranges through the mountains of Wyoming, Utah and Colorado. Unusually long tail. Otherwise similar to the Eastern Red Fox.

The High Sierra Red Fox (*Vulpes necator*) ranges through the High Sierras of California. Medium in size and similar to Eastern.

The Cascade Red Fox (*Vulpes cascadensis*) is found from the northern Sierra Nevadas of California through the Cascades of Oregon and Washington. A large variety in which the "black-cross" color phase appears unusually frequently. Short-tailed and light in color in normal phase.

The British Columbia Red Fox (*Vulpes alascensis abietorum*) is found in the interior of British Columbia northward into southeastern Alaska. Has a long slender head.

The Alaska Red Fox (*Vulpes alascensis alascensis*) ranges through northern Alaska. This is a large, long-tailed variety; with fiery red coloration; pelage long, soft and silky; ears small; distinctly black feet.

The Kenai Red Fox (*Vulpes kenaiensis*) is found on Kenai Peninsula, Alaska. Similar to Alaska Red.

The Kodiak Red Fox (*Vulpes harrimani*) is found on Kodiak Island, the Alaska Peninsula and Unimak Island. This is the largest of all the red fox, attaining a body length of 52 inches, and more on occasion. It has an unusually large and long-haired tail; pelage coarse, but very durable; hair on neck and shoulders unusually long; coloration duller and with less silkiness than Alaska Red Fox. Very plentiful in most areas of its range.

Of the Arctic Foxes there are seven different varieties, as here briefly described:

RED FOX

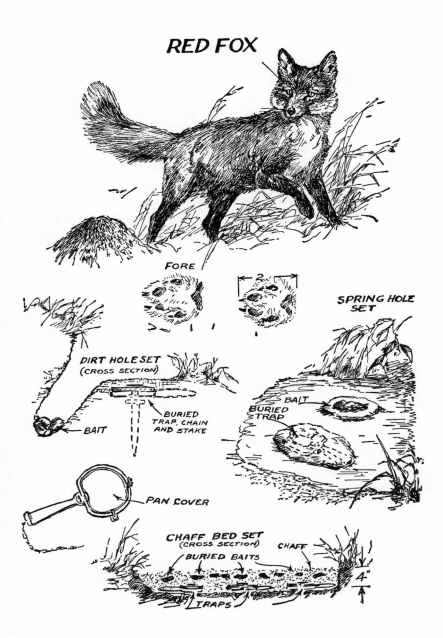

FORE

2

SPRING HOLE SET

DIRT HOLE SET
(CROSS SECTION)

BURIED TRAP, CHAIN AND STAKE

BAIT

BAIT

BURIED TRAP

PAN COVER

CHAFF BED SET
(CROSS SECTION)

BURIED BAITS

CHAFF

TRAPS

4"

The Arctic Fox (*Alopex lagopus lagopus*), the type variety, is strictly speaking an Old World species native to the Arctic region of both Asia and Europe, but extending across Bering Straits into Alaska. It is also known as the White Fox, Blue Fox and Polar Fox. It is smaller than the average Red Fox of the North, with shorter ears and shorter snout. The pelage is very thick and long; and the tail is particularly full and bushy, although shorter than in the reds. The sexes are colored alike and there is but little difference in their size. Total length averages about 30 inches. In summer the Arctic Fox is dark brown to slate color, with yellowish to whitish on the belly, sides of neck and flanks. In winter they are entirely pure white. There is a "blue" color phase—although the blue animals do not turn white in winter.

The Continental Arctic Fox (*Alopex lagopus innuitus*) is found throughout Arctic Alaska, mainly along the coastal regions. It is similar to the type variety, although generally slightly smaller.

The Pribilof Fox (*Alopex pribilofensis*) is found only on the Pribilof Islands in Bering Sea. In shape it resembles the Red Fox somewhat more than the Arctic, except that it is of the "white" variety, with the "blue" phase predominating.

The Hall Island Fox (*Alopex hallensis*) is found only on Hall Island, Bering Sea. A small variety resembling the Arctic Fox.

The Bering Island Fox (*Alopex beringensis*) is found on the Bering Island, Aleutian Islands, Alaska.

The Labrador Arctic Fox (*Alopex lagopus ungava*) is found from Arctic eastern Alaska across Arctic Canada to Labrador. There are no outward differences between this variety and the Continental Arctic Fox.

The Greenland Arctic Fox (*Alopex greenlandicus*) is found on Greenland. A large variety, otherwise similar to Labrador.

Of the Kit Foxes or Swifts there are six recognized varieties. But as these are all small in size and their pelts are of far less value in the fur trade, they are of comparatively little importance to the trapper. In size they range from a total length of 26 to about 38 inches; in coloration generally yellowish, with white-tipped and black-tipped hairs; yellowish brown back of ears and outer sides of legs; black spot on side of snout; tail less bushy, buff gray on top and yellower underneath, with black tip. Here, very briefly, are the several varieties: Kit Fox or Swift (*Vulpes velox velox*), the type variety, found from New Mexico northward into Saskatchewan; the Prairie Fox (*Vulpes velox hebes*) is found from North Dakota and Saskatchewan westward into southeastern British Columbia; the Long-eared Kit Fox (*Vulpes macrotis macrotis*) is found in southwestern California; the San Joaquin Kit Fox (*Vulpes macrotis mutica*) is found in the San Joaquin Valley, Calif.; the Desert Kit Fox (*Vulpes macrotis arsipus*) is found in the Mohave and Colorado deserts, Calif.; and the New Mexico Desert Fox (*Vulpes macrotis neomexicana*) is found in southern Arizona, New Mexico and southwestern Texas.

Of the Gray Foxes there are twelve recognized varieties; but what is true of the Kit Foxes is also the case in the grays. They are not of any great importance as a fur bearer. They are on the average somewhat smaller than the reds. In coloration they are grizzled gray and black, lighter on the sides; marked with brownish red about the ears, sides of neck and sides of front legs; blackish snout; tail heavily marked with black; cheeks and inside of ears white; black chin; and belly white to tawny. Males and females about same size. In spite of their relative unimportance as fur bearers, here they are: The Eastern Gray Fox (*Urocyon cinereoargenteus cinereoargenteus*), the type variety, ranges over eastern United States from Virginia into the New England States and west to the Great Lake Regions and northern Texas; the Northern Gray Fox (*Urocyon cinereoargenteus borealis*) is found in New Hampshire; the Florida Gray Fox (*Urocyon cinereoargenteus floridanus*) ranges from Florida to eastern Texas; the Wisconsin Gray Fox (*Urocyon cinereoargenteus ocythous*) is found in the upper Mississippi Valley; the Arizona Gray Fox (*Urocyon cinereoargenteus scotti*) is found in western Texas and New Mexico west into southern California; the California Gray Fox (*Urocyon cinereoargenteus californicus*) is found in southern California; the Redwood Gray Fox (*Urocyon cinereoargenteus sequoiensis*) is found from Lake County south to Monterey Bay, California; the Townsend Gray Fox (*Urocyon cinereoargenteus townsendi*) is found in northern California; the San Miguel Island Fox (*Urocyon littoralis littoralis*) is found on San Miguel Island, California; the Santa Cruz Island Fox (*Urocyon littoralis santa-*

cruzae) is found on Santa Cruz Island, California; the San Clemente Island Fox (*Urocyon clementae*) is found on San Clemente Island, California; and the Santa Catalina Island Fox (*Urocyon catalinae*) is found on the Santa Catalina Island, California.

Here also are a few statistics which give something of an idea of the abundance and distribution of foxes in North America. The figures are from official sources; however, due to the large number of foxes that are taken by hunters for pure sport, the figures are far from being complete. The total for the last season for which reports are available show 445,557 foxes reported as taken in 37 States, Alaska and the Pribilof Islands. Of this total, which represents foxes of all kinds and varieties, the largest number was taken in Texas, with 56,253; Michigan, 52,017; Wisconsin, 36,487; Ohio, 29,138; Missouri, 26,563; with Alaska well down the list with 14,705. The latest report from Canada shows a total of 267,863; of which Ontario reported 86,902, of which 22,985 were ranch raised; Quebec, 81,113, of which 41,400 were ranch raised; and Alberta, 59,533, of which 11,087 were ranch raised.

Not only are the various foxes quite different in color and size, but also in general habits. The red fox prefer moderately overgrown cover, although they do not regularly haunt heavy stands of timber nor the open brushless plains. The kit fox, however, spends much of its time on the open plains and prairies, is a burrow-dweller, and is less cunning than the other varieties. The gray fox is more of a warm climate animal, being found even in desert areas. It is also a forest-dweller and often climbs up into low trees. As its name implies, the Arctic fox is a dweller of the northern tundra wastes, beyond the tree limit. Its summers are spent along the coast or open tundra; but in winter it very frequently goes out on the sea ice to follow the polar bear and feed on what he leaves of the seals or walrus he kills. Unlike his relatives, the Arctic fox frequently stores up food for the lean weeks of winter. Large numbers of lemmings and other food are killed and piled in crevices in the rocks for this purpose. It is also cannibalistic, not hesitating to kill and eat one of its own kind that may be caught in a trap.

The feeding habits of all the foxes are fundamentally similar. Their menu is a very broad one, taking advantage of most anything in the way of mice, small rodents, small mammals, birds, rabbits or even fruit and berries which their particular haunts may afford. The Arctic fox adds fish, sea urchins or any carrion it can find on the beach or elsewhere.

Volumes could be written about the foxes and their trapping. For the purposes of this book the comments must be limited and stress will be put on those more specifically relating to the red and Arctic foxes.

Indications are that most foxes are strictly monogamous—pairs mate for life and they are faithful to each other at all times, which marks their most radical difference from dogs. As Ernest Thompson Seaton put it, "as far as the evidence goes, the fox is proven to have attained the highest level of animal marriage." (The sea otter is a possible exception.) This does not mean that pairs are always found together; but, they usually start running in pairs about the first of January; intensive courtship and connubiality begins along about early February in the southern regions and March in the north, and the young are born from the last of March to the first of May dependent upon the latitude. The pups number from one to eleven, with four or five as the average.

Red fox dens are often remodeled woodchuck burrows or recesses under the base of big trees; although extensive observations indicate that they sleep in the open all winter and retire to the dens principally to bear their young and as a last resort for safety from hunting hounds. The Arctic foxes generally dig their own burrows and are inclined to spend more time in them, often having fox villages where numbers of pairs live in close proximity. These latter are also a great deal more tidy and clean about their dens and their personal appearance than the reds. In its family life it is in most respects equal or superior to the primitive Eskimos inhabiting the same regions.

Both varieties do a lot of barking—if bark their voicing can be called. It is a pleasant little chirping bark. But they also are capable of other and far less attractive sounds—occasionally resembling a shriek or a scream.

Foxes are not nearly as difficult to trap as most inexperienced persons believe, and with certain obvious modifications, the rules for success are pretty much the same for all varieties.

Around farming sections, the "chaff bed" method of trapping can be used very successfully. To make such a set, select a place on slightly sloping ground in an unused or weed grown field, preferably near woods or brush land, and either find or make a depression in the ground 3 or 3½ feet in diameter and 4 or 5 inches deep. Make provision to drain this depression so as to prevent freezing. Fill the cavity slightly more than level with buckwheat chaff. If this is not available any dark colored chaff will do. Any earth removed should be taken away some distance and concealed. Smooth the chaff over level with the edges of the opening and bait with lard cracklings. Mix a quantity into the chaff and scatter some in the surrounding weeds. This material can be secured from any meat packing company or from almost any butcher. This bait is recommended because it has been cooked and will last much longer without becoming putrid.

This should all be done at least several weeks before you set the traps. Allow the foxes to come and dig out the bait repeatedly, rebait and smooth off the chaff with a stick or limb and go and come by the same route each time and leave as few signs of your presence as possible. On or about November 1st, when the fur is commencing to prime, set four traps, one on each of the four sides of the circle with the center of the pan about eight inches in from the edge of the chaff. Cover traps, chain and clog or drag with the chaff. Smooth over carefully and leave it as near the same in appearance as possible.

No. 2 traps should be used and either an iron grapple or a short wooden clog should be used so the fox will leave the bed as soon as caught and will not disturb the other traps or dig up the bed, but will be found fast in the brush nearby.

Use gloves in handling both bait and traps. A rainy morning is the best time to set the traps for the first trial. Always attend the sets in the morning, as this gives a number of hours for any human odors you may leave to disappear. Any farm boy can attend two or three of these sets before and after school, and if properly done will catch practically all the foxes in the vicinity. A few drops of good fox scent in the center of the bed will help.

If there are foxes traveling your trapping grounds, find out the places they go with greater regularity. Perhaps the fox follows the bottom of a gully, a cattle path or an old woods road. Or, maybe he travels the top of a ridgeback or along the sandy beach of a lake or stream. Probably he frequently visits an old orchard, sawdust pile or sandpit, or skirts along the edge of a swale. Locate all these places where foxes travel the most, for it is important to locate the fox sets on such regular routes of travel. The ability to locate suitable places for setting the traps is just about half the job done, the other work involved consists of the selection of equipment and taking precautions in making the set.

First-class traps are vitally important for success. The No. 2 Coil Spring was designed especially for fox. The No. 1½ or No. 2 Long Spring or the No. 2 Jump are particularly adaptable for catching this animal.

Fox traps should be free of oil and grease and all human or domestic odors. Boil your traps in a solution made by boiling soft maple bark, butternut bark or black walnut hulls in water, or if none of the above are available, use ordinary willow tops with a few hemlock or balsam boughs. This treatment gives traps a deep blue color, keeps them from rusting easily, and provides for quick powerful action without the use of oil or grease.

In the East where there are thousands of warm spring holes which never freeze even in the dead of winter, the water set is a very successful method for catching foxes; as a matter of fact, it has practically become standard with professional fox trappers in all parts of the East. This old and time-tested method is simple. The trap is set in the edge of the water with the pan just covered by a skim of water, and a flat sod or piece of moss that will just nicely fill the space between the open jaws is placed upon the pan to afford a dry place for the fox to step. Place the bait on another sod or moss-covered stone eight inches farther out in the water, cover bait with wet leaves, and put a few drops of fox scent around. The water set, when made in warm springs, is the best fox set for late fall trapping, when dirt sets are unreliable, due to the soil freezing, but certain precautions must be taken to make it bring home the bacon. The trap must be set next to smooth, dry shore that is nearly level with the water, as the fox will not climb down a bank to your set. The sod or moss on the pan should not be more than 4 or 4½ inches from the shore line.

Place trap, chain, clog or drag under water with the pan at or just above the water. Conceal everything but the pan with the water-soaked leaves and place moss over the pan. All this should be done while standing in the water and the shore should not be touched.

The stepping-stone set is another good water set. Sometimes these can be located where foxes have habitually used them for numerous seasons as means of crossing streams or other wet places on their regular routes. It is also quite practicable to create such places—but this should be done well in advance of trapping time. If you can find a fox route along the edge of a stream or across a swampy area, carry stones and make a stepping-stone crossing. If the stones are covered with moss or dirt, etc., so much the better. Where old logging roads come to and cross a shallow stream is an ideal place for this. In addition to the stepping-stone crossing also put a large stone, preferably flat-topped, out in the water about two steps distance from the other stones; and place an additional flat-topped stone between this larger stone and one of the crossing stones. This latter stone should be well covered with moss, etc., for it will be the one on which your trap will be set when the trapping season comes around; while the other larger one will be·used for the bait. The chances are that foxes will get in the habit of using the stepping-stones and become accustomed to seeing the other stones. When the time comes to use the set, it is best to approach the stones by walking in the water. Carefully remove the covering of moss on the trap stone; set your trap and re-arrange the moss, etc., to make it appear as closely as possible to its original appearance. Then place a bait and sprinkle some scent on the larger stone. In a section where foxes are fairly plentiful, a set such as this should account for several catches during the season.

If it is not convenient to find or make a stepping-stone layout across a stream (if the water is too deep or no stones are available), search for a log crossing or chop down a tree so that it will fall across the stream and form a natural bridge crossing. The traps are set on the ground at each side of the stream where the animals step on and off the log. If sand or fine earth is placed at these places where you intend to set your traps, you can tell by the tracks whether or not the bridge is being used and by what kind of animals. When the traps are set, the dropping of a branch or two in the proper spots will influence the animals to step in the proper spot.

Stepping-stones and log crossings as above described will be freely used by foxes, raccoons, wild cats and sometimes mink. Use good strong traps and a drag or drag hook so that the animals caught can get away from the location. If they are fastened permanently the disturbance they make is apt to cause other animals to avoid the crossing for a considerable time to come.

The successful trapper is the one who can adapt the best methods to conditions as he finds them. There are sections of country where numerous foxes are to be caught and yet none of the above kinds of sets can be made. Under such conditions the smelling-post set may solve your problem. Foxes are like coyotes, wolves and dogs in having certain places where they will habitually stop to lift-a-hind-leg. Even a stray dog will run straight to such a place and leave his evidence of having been there. In the case of fox trapping these smelling-posts or urinating-posts can quite easily be created. But they must be close to a trail or path known to be regularly used by the animals on their routes of travel.

Select an open spot where there is an unobstructed view for 30 or 40 feet. In the center of this and a few feet to one side of the trail plant a small evergreen bush about six to ten inches high. Sometimes such a "prop" can be found. It should, however, stand out prominently without other brush or tall grass around it. This is to be the smelling-post. Make an excavation on the trail side of it to take your trap, together with the drag-hook and chain. Carefully dispose of all the surplus earth removed and see that the finished set looks as natural as though no trap had been set there. Sprinkle a little fox urine on the smelling-post each time you visit the trap, especially after rains. These sets are far more effective if they are established and put into use a considerable length of time before the trapping season opens and the first trap is laid. Such smelling-posts can be placed within a quarter of a mile apart, as the foxes are apt to stop at each such place they pass.

Incidentally, the one way to get the stuff to drop on these sets is to take a fox home alive and put him in a cage with a tin bottom tilted so that the urine will drain into a receptacle from which it can periodically be collected and bottled. Otherwise, the urine can easily be removed from the bodies of the foxes you catch, after they have been skinned. One of the greatest dangers in making a smelling-post set is that too much scent is apt to be used, which will cause the visiting foxes to dig rather than just tarry to lift-a-leg.

Probably the most common and one of the most successful sets used by fox trappers is what is called the dirt-hole or baited-hole set. It also takes a lot of other fur bearers, such as skunk, raccoon, mink, etc. It also has the added advantage of being simple and easy to make.

The dirt-hole set is nothing more than an imitation of what is done by an animal when it buries part of a rabbit or other piece of meat which it cannot at the time eat and will be cached to be dug up at a later time. The advantage to the trapper is that such a cache is fair gain for any animal that happens to find it—for thievery among animals is considered fair practice.

A fairly open field or a gently sloping hillside, where the ground is easily dug, is an ideal location. Droppings, tracks or scratchings will tell you if it is frequented by foxes. Select a spot and approach it from down-hill. Lay your piece of oil-cloth to kneel on, and also place your trap and other equipment on this. The trap should already have the jaws set and be all ready to place in position. Incidentally, in setting the trap *never* hold it on your knee to do so—instead, place it on the ground and put your foot on the spring and never handle the traps without gloves. You'd be surprised how much human odor can become attached to them by careless handling.

Dig a hole about three inches in diameter and six inches deep. The hole should slant at about 45 degrees; and the dirt spread out below the opening. A trowel can be used for the digging. In the dirt excavated carefully dig out a place for the trap. This should be so that the trap when placed will be about four or five inches from the lower edge of the hole, and when finally covered not more than an inch or two higher than the lower edge of the hole.

Drive the stake into the ground directly in the center of where the trap will be placed; coil the chain around on top; and place your trap on top.

Covering the trap in this set is very important. Soft dry leaves, grass, moss or even cotton are frequently placed under the pan to keep out the dirt which is later sifted over the whole trap. In any event, be sure that the trap pan will be free to go down when the fox steps on it and the jaws will be able to come up through the covering. As a precaution against freezing, rain or moisture, a large leaf or waxed paper, slit to go around the trigger of the trap and then tucked over the pan and under the jaws, permits free action. Some trappers use pieces of thin canvas or oil cloth, cut to fit inside the jaws—although waxed paper is less apt to freeze to the trap.

Then sift dirt over your set until it is completely covered and gives a perfectly natural appearance. Even a few small leaves scattered over the top adds to its natural appearance.

The hole is of course baited with some natural food. A small piece of tainted meat should be placed in the bottom of the hole and lightly covered with dirt. Other baits which can be used are cheese, canned salmon, fish or most anything that gives off a strong odor. Some trappers add scent; and some use only scent.

The set should not be approached closer than necessary to see if anything has been caught; although scent should be added about every three to five days in cold weather and every ten days in milder weather.

The fact that a fox is caught at one of these sets does not mean the set cannot be used again, even if the trapped animal tears things up pretty badly. In fact, such a circumstance seems to improve it. But care should be taken to avoid any blood being dropped there. Remove the fox and carry it a safe distance away before killing it. The set should then be put in order for another set.

In summer, make conical mounds of dirt about twenty inches high along runways that foxes frequent the most, or use ant hills where they are available. A few days in advance of the trapping season, hollow out a hole on the peak of each mound or ant hill and place therein a strong steel trap equipped with drag hook and long chain, concealing these appendages directly under the trap. Now stuff a bunch of rubbed up dry leaves under the trap pan to prevent dirt getting beneath it and cover all with fine dirt. Two or three days after the traps are set, place the carcass of a skunk, coon or porcupine near each set or about fifteen feet from the mound and fasten these baits down to prevent other animals from dragging them away. Or, if the mound is located at about this distance from a small evergreen tree with dense foliage, it is best to hide the bait among the boughs six or eight feet from the ground. The fox will invariably jump upon the mound to look at the bait from a safe distance, and if a large powerful trap like the No. 3 Victor or Oneida Jump Trap is used a catch is always likely. This is an exceptionally good fox set, dog and stock proof. Small worthless animals like squirrels and rabbits seldom get fast and spoil the sets, and it is equally good for bare ground or light snow.

It is best to use rubber gloves when handling traps. Rubber footwear is also a worthwhile precaution. If you go to your traps in an auto, take a few extra moments to wipe the bottoms on the grass after getting out, or wash them in a stream if possible, to remove any possible oil, grease or other strong scents which may otherwise be left wherever you make a step.

Trapping foxes in the snow and sub-zero temperature is hard work. The difficulty is not so much in getting the game to come to your sets, but in keeping the traps in such working condition that they will catch him when he steps on the pan. Drifting snow and freezing have caused a lot of headaches to northern trappers. There is nothing more provoking than to find a fox track right on top of the pan of a frozen and unsprung trap. There is also the disadvantage that baits and scents are far less effective at low temperatures; and during the severe winter weather the animals are inclined to restrict their traveling to the more sheltered, timbered lowlands.

Many of the temperate climate sets can be adapted to low-temperature districts. The mound set is an example. A variation of this is to place your bait in such a position that the fox will hop up onto a big log lying conveniently close to get an elevated view of the situation. Usually the trap can be placed near the end of such a log.

The smelling-post set is also good for cold weather use; as are also the stepping-stone and the log crossing sets.

Foxes like to follow the shorelines of rivers and lakes when they are frozen and they can be taken on these sort of routes by sets made right in the ice. Select a point of land where a tree lies projecting out from the shore, where the fox will have to go around it. Dig out a basin in the ice, of sufficient size to hide your trap and grapple. Set the trap and cover the pan with stout waxed paper or a canvas pad; fill around the trap with snow; and sprinkle soft snow over the whole set until it is flush with the surrounding ice. The snow on top of the pan should not be more than enough to cover it. Properly made this set, when finished, resembles nothing more than a snow-filled break in the ice. It has the further advantage that the snow will sweep over it on the smooth ice and not drift-cover it. A dead limb can be placed on either side, to cause the fox to step in the right place—and some scent sprinkled on the sticks will aid in the general purpose for which the effort is expended.

Although no mean antagonist in the contest of wits, the fox really has but little chance against the superior brain of the skilled fox trapper. While their keen sense of smell will often detect the danger, more times it is what they see that makes them suspicious. They can be caught at a set that reeks of man odor, when the set is properly made and baited, but will swerve around a little disturbance on their run-way, even though it contains no human odor.

Simple sets, made quickly and with the least possible fresh signs, generally land the foxes; while elaborate sets, with a lot of fussing and treading around, are generally failures.

Fox pelts should always be cured flesh side out and turned fur side out when cured. The use of properly shaped fur stretchers is very important, as properly shaped and cured skins will bring better prices than those carelessly done. Dry fox skins in a well ventilated place, away from artificial heat or sunlight.

CHAPTER XIV

THE COYOTE AND WOLF

THE coyotes and the wolves are the wild dogs of America. They have both figured prominently in legend and story, for they come about as close to representing the "wilderness" of this continent, as any other wild animal. There was a time when one or the other of their several varieties were found in practically every section of North America. In Colonial times there was even a bounty for their killing on Long Island. Today the wolves are practically extinct in most sections of the United States, although they still exist in considerable numbers in a good many parts of northern Canada and Alaska. But still the wily coyote persists to survive in most of the less-populated sections of our West and Southwest.

They are all carnivorous by preference and among the most destructive predators on this continent. No animal, except the bear and mountain lion, is safe from the destructive attack of a hungry pack of wolves; although their danger to man has been somewhat exaggerated.

To the trapper-naturalist, the awesome call of the coyote, or even the howl of the wolf, on a quiet evening or moonlit night deep in the wilderness, is one of the most eerie but primitively pleasant of all the sounds he hears. It inspires both meditation and challenge to his own skill as a hunter and trapper.

The coyotes of North America are divided into the following eight scientifically recognized varieties:

The Northern Coyote or Brush Wolf (*Canis latrans*) ranges over the northern prairies and bordering woodlands of Iowa and Minnesota westward to the edge of the Rocky Mountains as far north as central Alberta. This is a small, slender wolf somewhat resembling a shepherd dog, with long, heavy pelage and large bushy tail. In coloration it is a mixture of gray, buff and black; snout, ears and outer sides of legs yellowish; tip of tail black; belly whitish. The males are larger than females. A large male will have a total length of up to 55 inches or sometimes more, and weigh up to 50 pounds.

The Prairie Coyote or Prairie Wolf (*Canis nebracensis nebracensis*), sometimes called the Nebraska Coyote, ranges from Colorado northward into Canada. It resembles the previous variety but is smaller and paler in color, with fewer black tipped hairs.

The Great Basin Coyote (*Canis lestes*) is found from central British Columbia southward through the higher lands of the Great Basin, the Sierra Nevadas and the Rocky Mountains to the Mexican Border. This is a large coyote, with large ears and tail.

The Texas Coyote (*Canis nebracensis texensis*) ranges from the Gulf coast region of Texas northward into Oklahoma. It is medium in size; and in coloration buffy brown, with reddish snout, legs and feet yellowish.

The Small-toothed Coyote (*Canis microdon*) is found in the arid regions of the lower Rio Grande regions of Texas southward into Mexico. It is a small variety, dark in coloration and with very small teeth.

The Mearns Coyote (*Canis mearnsi*) is found in southern Arizona. It is small in size; coloration bright and rich.

The Desert Coyote (*Canis estor*) is found in the desert regions of Utah, Nevada and California. This is the smallest of the coyotes and is pale in color.

The San Joaquin Valley Coyote (*Canis ochropus*) is found in the San Joaquin Valley, California. It is a small variety, much more darkly colored than most varieties.

According to the latest figures compiled by the United States Fish and Wild Life Service, the largest number of coyotes were taken in the State of Kansas where 26,853 were trapped during 1945; then comes New Mexico, with 20,000; Idaho, 15,850; Washington, 9,144. In Canada the two top Provinces are Alberta, with a catch of 30,886 and Saskatchewan, 26,785. These figures are undoubtedly incomplete and far below the total of animals actually taken. The data is based entirely on the reports of trappers, and do not include the large numbers taken by hunters or trappers who made no official report.

The Wolves of North America are divided into nine scientifically recognized varieties:

The Gray or Timber Wolf (*Canis nubilus*) ranges over the Great Plains of Iowa, Nebraska, Kansas, Wyoming, the Dakotas and eastward to the Great Lakes. This is also sometimes called the Buffalo Wolf or Lobo—for it was the wolf that once followed and preyed upon the buffalo in the days when they roamed the Great Plains in great numbers. Now scarce and even unknown in some sections where he once was plentiful; he is a big fellow attaining a total length of 66 inches or more and attaining a weight of well over a hundred pounds. In coloration his general pattern is gray sprinkled with black (salt-and-pepper), with a brownish muzzle, and yellowish legs and belly.

The Oklahoma Wolf (*Canis frustror*) is found in Oklahoma and is a small variety with a reddish tinge.

The Texan Red Wolf (*Canis rufus*) is found in southern Texas. This also is a small variety, reddish brown in color and with much black on top of the tail.

The Florida Wolf (*Canis floridanus*) is found in Florida. It is light buff in general color sprinkled with black on back; rusty muzzle, legs and feet. There is also a black phase.

The Eastern Timber Wolf (*Canis lycaon*) ranges through the northern parts of the northeastern United States and eastern Canada. It is reddish brown in general coloration with black-tipped hairs on back.

The Puget Sound Wolf (*Canis gigas*) is found in the Puget Sound area. It is large in size and reddish brown, heavily sprinkled with black; and a short tail.

The Northern Gray Wolf (*Canis occidentalis*) is found throughout the timbered areas of northwestern Canada and

WOLF and COYOTE

FORE FOOT PRINTS

WOLF — COYOTE — 5" — 3"

STREAM SET

BAIT — TRAPS — BURNT MEAT SET — BURIED TRAPS

Alaska. It is a very large wolf, very gray in color. There is a black phase, which is sometimes bluish in color. Weight up to 150 pounds.

The Mt. McKinley Timber Wolf (*Canis pambasileus*) is found in the region of Mt. McKinley and vicinity, Alaska. This too is a very large, heavy wolf. The color varies from grizzled light gray or dirty white, sprinkled with black, to almost solid black.

The White or Tundra Wolf (*Canis tundrarum*) is found throughout the Barren Lands and tundras of Arctic Canada and Alaska. Also very large in size. In coloration light buff to white with faint sprinkling of dusky gray on back and tail; light brown on muzzle. A big, rangy brute, very handsome in a very primitive way.

According to government figures there was a total of only 1,015 wolves caught by trappers in the entire United States during the 1945-46 season. The catch in Alaska adds another 290. The largest number for any State was 413 for Minnesota; Iowa was next with 388; Oklahoma, 85; Michigan, 61. In Canada a total of 10,181 wolves were trapped in 1944—of which 6,680 were taken in Manitoba; British Columbia, 1,280; Saskatchewan, 625; Northwest Territories, 531. These figures, of course, do not include those taken by hunters or by trappers who did not make a report on same, but it does give the best available estimate of the present day range of these animals. But just to think—there once was bounty on wolves that were taken on Long Island—where many were caught within what is now the city limits of New York City!

Both coyotes and wolves are primarily carnivorous, preferring meat for their dinner table. The coyote's natural food is most any small wild animals they are fortunate enough to catch, as well as birds, snakes, lizards, even insects and they like an occasional feast on fruit—all depending on the natural food resources of the district in which they live. They have also learned to like many of the things that the farmer and rancher depends upon for his livelihood. Poultry and lamb are particularly to the coyote's liking, and he will even make midnight raids upon the farmer's store of fresh milk if he can find a way to get at it. As for the wolf, he goes in for a little more big-time banquets of deer, moose, caribou, antelope and domestic stock. A lone old he-wolf is capable of pulling down a pretty good size animal single handed, often resorting to hamstringing (chewing apart the tendons in the back of the leg) as a preliminary step, if they cannot be pulled down by brute force. When necessary, particularly in winter, they will run in packs for the purpose of pulling down full grown big game. The old-time Buffalo Wolf habitually traveled in packs in search of buffalo that had been wounded by Indian's arrows or personal combat; and when such was located their favorite method of attack was to tear the buffalo's face to shreds, putting out their eyes in the process and then swarm all over the unfortunate beast and literally eat the animal alive until it fell to the ground from loss of blood.

Coyotes and wolves today make serious inroads on the stocks of sheep and lambs, cattle, pigs, and poultry, as well as on the wild game mammals and ground-nesting and insectivorous birds. Wherever these predatory animals occur in large numbers, they are a source of worry and loss to stockmen, farmers, and sportsmen. The coyote is by far the most persistent of the predators of the western range country. Moreover, it is a carrier of rabies, or hydrophobia. The coyote has also been found to be a carrier of tularemia, a disease of wild rabbits and other rodents that is transmissible and sometimes fatal to human beings.

The steel trap, in Victor and Newhouse sizes 3 and 4 for coyotes and Newhouse sizes 4½ and 14 for wolves (114 in Alaska), are all proper for capturing these large predators. The 3N Victor, a trap made to meet the exacting specifications of the Fish and Wildlife Service, is especially recommended for coyotes.

On the open range coyotes and wolves have "scent posts," or places where they come to urinate. The animals usually establish these posts along their runways on stubble of range grasses, on bushes, or possibly on some old bleached-out carcasses. Where ground conditions are right for good tracking, these scent posts may be detected from the toenail scratches on the ground made by the animals after they have urinated. This habit of having scent posts and of scratching is similar to the habit common to dogs.

Finding these scent posts is of prime importance, for it is at such points that traps should be set. If such posts cannot be found, then one can be readily established, if the travel way of the coyote or wolf has been definitely ascertained, by dropping scent (of the kind described later) on a few clusters of weeds, spears of grass or stubble of low brush. The trap should then be set at this point. Any number of such scent stations can thus be placed along a determined wolf or coyote travel way.

Time consumed in finding a wolf or coyote scent post is well spent, for the success of a trap set depends upon its location.

Places where carcasses of animals killed by wolves and coyotes or of animals that have died from natural causes have lain a long time, offer excellent spots for setting traps, for wolves and coyotes often revisit these carcasses. It is always best to set the traps a few yards away from the carcasses at weeds, bunches of grass, or low stubble of bushes. Other good situations are at the intersection of two or more trails, around old bedding grounds of sheep, and at water holes on the open range.

Traps used should be clean, with no foreign odor. In making a set, a hole the length and width of the trap with jaws open is dug. While digging, the trapper should stand or kneel on a "setting cloth," about three feet square, made of canvas or of a piece of calf hide.

If canvas is used, the human scent may be removed by previously burying it in an old manure pile. The dirt removed from the hole dug to bed the trap is placed on the setting cloth. The trap is then dropped into the hole and firmly bedded so as to rest perfectly level.

Instead of using digging tools, some hunters bed the trap where the ground is loose, as in sandy loam, by holding it at its base and with a circular motion working it slowly into the ground even with or slightly below the surface and then removing the dirt from under the pan before placing the trap pad.

The next stage is the careful burying of the trap and building up of a so-called shoulder around and under the pan. This should be so built that, when it is completed, the shape of the ground within the jaws of the trap represents an inverted cone, in order to give a foundation for the pan cover, commonly called the "trap pad." The trap pad may be made of canvas, of old "slicker cloth," or even of a piece of ordinary wire fly screen or worn out window blinds, cut into the proper shape. The trap pad to be effective must contain no foreign odor that might arouse the suspicion of wolf or coyote.

In placing the trap pad over the pan and onto the shoulders of the dirt built up for carrying it, the utmost care must be taken to see that no rock, pebble, or dirt slips under the pan, which would prevent the trap from springing. With the trap pad in place, the entire trap is carefully covered with the remaining portion of earth on the setting cloth.

Cover traps at least half an inch deep with dry dust if possible. It is well to have the covered surface over the trap a little lower than the surrounding ground. All surplus earth on the setting cloth not needed for covering the trap should be taken a good distance away.

A few drops of scent are now applied to the weed, cluster of grass, or stubble used as the scent post. A scent tested and successfully used by government hunters is made as follows:

Put into a bottle or glass jar the urine and the gall of a wolf or a coyote, depending on which is to be trapped; and also the anal glands, which are situated under the skin on either side of the vent and resemble small pieces of bluish fat. If these glands cannot be readily found, the whole anal parts may be used. To every 3 ounces of the mixture add 1 ounce of glycerine, to give it body and to prevent too rapid evaporation, and 1 grain of corrosive sublimate to keep it from spoiling.

Let the mixture stand several days, then shake well and scatter a few drops on weeds or ground six or eight inches from the place where the trap is set. The farther from the travel way the trap is set, the more scent will be needed. A little of the scent should be rubbed on the trapper's gloves and shoe soles to conceal the human odor.

If the animals become "wise" to this kind of scent, an effective fish scent may be prepared in the following way:

Grind the flesh of sturgeon, eels, suckers, carp, or other oily variety of coarse fish in a sausage mill, place in strong tin or iron cans, and leave in a warm place or even temperature to decompose thoroughly. Provide can with a vent to allow escape of gas (otherwise there is danger of explosion), but screen the aperture with a cloth to prevent flies depositing eggs. This scent may be used within three days after it is prepared, but it is more lasting and penetrating after a lapse of 30 days. It is also very attractive to livestock, and its use on heavily stocked ranges is not recommended, as cattle are attracted to such scent stations and will spring the traps.

The place where a wolf or coyote has thus been caught affords an excellent location for a reset after the animal has been removed from the trap. This is due to the natural scent dropped by the animal while in the trap.

It is always advisable to wear gloves while setting traps and to use them for no other purpose than for trap setting.

A good general rule to follow in the selecting of any bait or scent, no matter what fur-bearing animal you are trapping, is not to use *anything* that is not native to the district in which you are trapping and that is not familiar to the animal you are trapping. There are some exceptions to this, such as canned salmon, sardines, catnip, etc.—but in spite of these exceptions it's a pretty good general rule to follow.

It is also well to remember, incidentally, that the coyote in certain districts at least is subject to and a carrier of the dangerous "rabies" or hydrophobia as well as tularemia, both of which can be transmitted to humans and often prove fatal. It should also be remembered by farmers and livestock-raisers, who are be-damned by the depredations of coyotes or wolves, that careful experiments by government predatory control agents, as well as others, have proven that trapping is the most effective method of capturing these animals.

Many trappers use two or more traps at the sets they make. The principle is that two feet each caught in a trap is more apt to hold these animals.

The matter of scent is also a problem of trial, error and success. If one method doesn't appear to work, try something else, until you hit the right one. There are no cut-and-dried rules in trapping. It's the trapper who studies and skillfully best analyzes the situations on his own trapping grounds who gets the best results. Most highly successful trappers develop methods of their own, which are best adapted to their own country; although practically all of these are fundamentally based upon a limited number of common methods.

In isolated areas away from live stock the trail set can be used to advantage. On a trail being used by coyotes or wolves, if you can find a place where it cuts sharply around a protruding large rock, base of a tree or prominent root over which the animal must step, dig your trap in with the pan where he will step the next time he passes that way. Often a skillfully placed obstruction would help, a small tree limb or piece of brush dropped in the trail. This requires as much skill and understanding of the game, as the actual setting of the trap.

No matter what type of set you decide to make, look the place over carefully before you disturb it and know exactly what you are going to do *before* you start.

Many coyote and wolf trappers prefer to use a drag on their traps, so the caught animal will quickly leave the location without disturbing it; although it has been repeatedly proven that the spot where an animal has been caught and has "scented up" the location is a strong attraction for others of his kind.

Along a stream where the flood waters have cut a sharp channel and there are cut banks, the coyotes will have certain places where they jump down when going for water or traveling their regular routes. If such a spot is found, dig your trap in where you figure the animal will put his feet in approaching the edge of the bank in trying to look down to see where and what the scent may be.

In country where there is little vegetation a scent post can be established by planting a small sage brush or even an old dead stick. Fastening a small piece of rabbit fur or sheep wool to such a scent post and saturating it with coyote or wolf urine, or whatever call scent you are using, is advantageous. Here again the traps must be placed and carefully concealed where the prospective game will walk into them; and here again is an excellent place to use the fake imprint of animal foot-prints right on the spot over the pan of traps.

In making any and all of these sets it is *highly important not to leave any human scent or signs*. Use a kneeling pad; rubber foot-wear and gloves; lay everything you are using on the kneeling pad and not on the surrounding ground; do not spring and set your traps by holding them on your own knee and have them already sprung and ready to place before approaching the particular spot; use a virgin piece of brush or bunch of long grass to brush out all unnatural marks in the ground covering the traps; straighten up any vegetation pressed down where you have knelt or walked, in the same manner; and scatter a few wild leaves etc., on top of the fresh earth. You cannot be too careful in making the place appear natural when you leave it.

A good water set is to place a large flat stone about five or six feet out from the shore of a shallow pond or back water in a stream. Some growing vegetation should be put on it; and fasten on this the carcass of a rabbit, or other native game. Put some scent on the carcass or the sod; and place your traps in the water about six or eight inches from the bait. Some trappers prefer to put the traps near the shore; but this depends on the location. If there is a small point of dry land projecting out towards the bait, the shore line set is more apt to bring results. For sets of this kind the water should not be more than two or three inches deep; and in making such sets the trapper should of course approach the location through the water, entering and leaving it some distance from the set. If the bottom is muddy or soft, be careful to wipe out the imprints of your tracks as you leave the location. This can easily be done with one foot or the limb of a tree, as you back away.

Coyotes and wolves are attracted by the odor of scorched meat. Burn the carcass of a skinned rabbit or any other small native game and partly bury it six to ten feet off a trail. Select a spot for this where you know where the animals will leave the trail to approach the bait; and set your traps at the place between the trail and the bait where you feel most certain the prospective game will be most apt to step in approaching. Another method is to use a fresh carcass for bait; and after the bait and traps are all in position, pile some dead brush and leaves on top of both the bait and the traps and set it on fire. See that the fire consumes all of the brush and leaves, leaving only undisturbed ashes over both bait and traps. No other bait or scent is needed. Also a drag is best for this set—for re-use of the location.

The sets described here are by no means the only ones that will take coyotes and wolves, although they are all methods which have proven successful among trappers· over long periods of application and most anyone can use them efficiently with careful effort. Ideas for other types of sets can be gained from types of sets used for other fur bearers, and adapting same to your own situations. The most important thing of all is to be a close observer and keen student of the animals that inhabit your own district, and by so doing you can anticipate what the animals are in the habit of doing and how they will react to the methods you may decide to use in trapping them. In this, as in all types of trapping, being a good naturalist is the first requirement of being a successful trapper.

Both coyote and wolf skins should be case skinned. The tail should not be split, although the tail bone must of course be pulled out. An ordinary clothes-pin is a good accessory for pulling out tail bones. Leave the feet on, although the claws can be cut off. The pelts can be stretched fur side out, but make sure that the skin is free of all fat. The patented wire stretcher, adjustable to size, can be used, or wood stretchers can be made of ⅜ or ½ inch boards, sandpapered smooth. In warm weather it may be found nesessary to rub a little salt into the ears and skin side of the front legs.

CHAPTER XV

THE MARTEN

THE marten is one of the three most valuable of all North American fur bearers—and one of the easiest to capture by the trapper who has a working knowledge of the animal's habits. Once very plentiful in many of the colder, mountainous and wooded sections of this continent, it has been among the first to disappear before the onmarch of civilization and is now comparatively scarce except in rather remote sections of its former range.

There are eleven scientifically recognized varieties of the Marten (*Martes americana* and related forms) in North America—some of which are today exceedingly scarce or almost extinct. They are:

The American Marten (*Martes americana americana*) which ranges intermittently through the mountainous and timbered regions of eastern North America from Virginia westward to Minnesota and northward to the shores of Hudson Bay and Labrador. It is weasel-like in form and the body is a little smaller than that of the average house-cat; with richly soft pelage and bushy tail and ears prominently broad and rounded. In coloration it is found in various shades of rich yellowish brown, mixed with dark brown hairs; darker brown on legs and tail; ears generally edged with whitish; and belly somewhat lighter, with a bright buff area on throat and chest. The average total length is around 23 to 26 inches.

The Newfoundland Marten (*Martes atrata*) is found only in Newfoundland. This is a deep chocolate colored variety.

The North Labrador Marten (*Martes brumalis*) is found in northern Labrador. It is larger and darker than the American Marten.

The Hudson Bay Marten (*Martes americana abieticola*) ranges from the western shore of Hudson Bay westward into Saskatchewan and northward about as far as timber goes. It is generally somewhat larger than the American Marten and inclined to be somewhat darker in color.

The Rocky Mountain Marten (*Martes caurina origenes*) is found through the southern Rocky Mountains from New Mexico northward through Colorado. This variety is peculiarly different in coloration from other varieties, in that the brown on its back is considerably darker in the middle part and head and paling down the sides; belly, chest and throat blotched with buff; and ears not edged with whitish.

The Sierra Marten (*Martes caurina sierrae*) is found in the Sierra Nevadas, California. It is a small pale-colored variety.

The British Columbia Marten (*Martes americana abietinoides*) is found in the Selkirk and Gold Ranges of interior British Columbia. It is a small variety, with grizzled gray on head.

The Pacific Marten (*Martes caurina caurina*) is found in the mountainous coastal regions of British Columbia southward into northern California. This is a pale colored variety, medium in size.

The Queen Charlotte Marten (*Martes nesophila*) was originally found on Queen Charlotte Islands, British Columbia, and is today apparently extinct.

The Alaska Marten (*Martes americana actuosa*) is found from northern British Columbia northward through Alaska and Yukon as far as the timbered areas extend and eastward to the range of the Hudson Bay Marten. It is a large variety, rather pale in color, becoming grayish on shoulders and head.

The Kenai Marten (*Martes americana kinaiensis*) is found on the Kenai Peninsula, Alaska. It is comparatively small in size, with long tail and dark in color, often with no yellow spot on throat and belly generally darker than back.

The latest government records say that the total annual catch of marten for the entire United States was 2,954. Of these the State of Washington reported 1,233; Oregon, 867; Alaska, 453. The latest report for Canada is 19,530—of which British Columbia reports 11,739; Quebec, 2,853; Yukon, 2,024. It may also be interesting as well as significant to point out that equally reliable reports for the year 1864 give the total number of marten skins taken in North America, exclusive of Russian North America (Alaska) as 130,000; and for Siberia and Alaska an additional 109,000. Incidentally, the average auction sale price for marten in 1864 was $7.60 apiece, and in 1944 the *average price* for all marten skins taken in the Province of Alberta was $55.06.

The favorite native haunts of the marten are thick old-growth forests of evergreen, especially where there are plenty of dead trees among which they can hunt the mice, chipmunks, squirrels, rabbits and grouse which constitute their favorite food. Martens live among the trees very much like squirrels and are almost as expert as climbers. When seen among the tree-tops, racing from limb to limb and leaping across open spaces from one tree to another, the average person who is not particularly keen of eye or familiar with these handsome fur bearers is very apt to mistake them for large squirrels. On the ground they are equally agile and are capable of tracking down and capturing rabbits with the skill of a fox. They have a particularly good sense of smell and they will trail a rabbit or hare, nose to earth, like a well trained dog; then, upon sighting the quarry, make a wild dash. If the first dash is not successful, the marten will merely drop his nose to the ground and begin trailing again, knowing very confidently that success will be the ultimate end of his efforts.

The marten is so agile and clever both on the ground and in the tree-tops that he is generally able to escape from or protect himself against all natural enemies. Now and then, however, one is taken by the fisher, and possibly by a lynx or great horned owl.

It has been observed by woodsmen and marten trappers of long and extensive experience that the martens rather mysteriously become exceedingly scarce or almost disappear from all parts of

MARTEN

FORE

HIND

1 1/2"

BAIT

LEANING POLE SET

BAIT

TREE TRUNK SET

SPIKES

their native haunts about every eight or ten years—much as the ruffed grouse are known to disappear. Investigation has not proven, however, that this is the result of any disease or parasite, as in the case of the grouse. They are also much more difficult to trap just prior to these periods of scarcity.

The favorite "nest" of the marten is in a hole in a tree high above the ground; and they have a habit of lying with only one side of their face protruding from such a hole, while their keen little eyes skillfully observe whatever is moving about in the surrounding woods. Under such circumstances it takes an eagle-eyed woodsman to catch a glimpse of them, as they disappear like a flash of light. But in the late afternoon they can be seen moving about on the ground in search of supper. If a person is reasonably certain of the location of a marten nest and will take a stand in still-hunter fashion in the late afternoon and wait long enough, he is pretty certain to get a good look at one of them. If one sits perfectly still, they are apt to come within a few yards—but the slightest movement and they will disappear as if by magic.

In mountainous rocky country they often live in crevices among the ledges or a large crack in the face of a cliff.

Under normal circumstances the marten is a hardy and rather prolific creature. The young are born quite early in the spring, sometimes around the middle of April even in the northern zones; and they are as many as six kittens, or even more, to a litter.

While most fur-bearing animals will move their native haunts a short distance because of the presence of human beings, the marten will really get out of the country when a cabin is built or there is any evidence of civilization moving in. This does not mean that the tracks of a trapper through his domain will give the marten the moving urge—but he definitely does not like humans.

The tracks of the marten are very similar to those of the mink. They are normally made in pairs, with a distance of from 18 to 36 inches between jumps. The males are somewhat larger than the females. They leave but little sign of their presence, even when there is snow on the ground.

The cubby set is the most popular method used by most marten trappers. They seem to lack much of the suspicion of most fur bearers and they will walk right into an uncovered trap. The cubby can be constructed in most any manner which is natural to the situation. It can merely be a small pen made of sticks or stones placed against the base of a tree, covered over on top of course. The No. 1½ trap will hold the marten, although the No. 2 is safer in regions where a fisher is also apt to be caught. The trap is placed at the entrance of the cubby, either bare or covered lightly with natural camouflage of leaves, grass or whatever covers the surrounding ground. For bait use whatever you can procure which is to the marten's liking and is found in his particular habitat—rabbit, squirrel, venison, grouse etc. Some marten trappers also use lures of fish oil, muskrat musk or beaver castor. The bait does not have to be large and is generally covered with a sprinkling of small sticks or leaves.

In districts where snowfall is heavy and it is impracticable to use the cubby set, just drive a couple of spikes into a big spruce tree or build a small platform about three or four feet off the ground or snow-level; and place the bare trap on this, with the chain fastened to the tree in such a way that when the animal is caught and falls, it will be clear of the ground. Fasten your bait to the tree just above the trap.

The leaning pole set is also used extensively. There are several variations of this. You can fasten your bait to a tree; lean the pole against the tree with the top just below the bait; and the trap is fastened near the top of the pole. Another version is to lean the pole through the low crotch of a tree, with the upper end protruding three or four feet beyond. The bait is fastened to the upper end of the pole and the trap, placed between the bait and the crotch of the tree.

The marten is always skinned, cased and stretched with the fur side out. The tail should not be split, although the vertebrae should be pulled out. Leave the feet and claws on the skin.

CHAPTER XVI

THE FISHER

THE fisher is the royal crown prince of all fur-bearing animals in North America—and just about as scarce, in the United States at least. During the 1944-'45 trapping season only two fishers were officially recorded as having been caught in the entire U.S.A.—one in California and one in New Hampshire. That makes pretty slim hunting for a trapper who might have the poor judgment to specialize in catching these animals. In Canada, however, the latest official records report a total of 3,303 skins taken in the 1943-'44 trapping season—of which 1,097 were taken in Ontario; Quebec, 924; British Columbia, 700. The records for 1864 give a total of 12,500 for North America. All of which seems to prove that the fisher is today a pretty scarce fur bearer and never has been plentiful. That is one reason why its pelt brings the highest price of all our natural fur bearers; the other is that it is, in the opinion of many, the most beautiful.

There are only two scientifically recognized varieties of the fisher in North America.

Fisher (*Marpes pennanti pennanti*) formerly ranged from the mountainous regions of Virginia northward into Quebec and westward in the timbered and mountainous sections into the Rocky Mountains as far south as northern Wyoming and the Pacific coast of British Columbia, and northward through Maine and into northern Quebec. It is the smaller of the two varieties, although a full grown male will measure up to 36 or 38 inches and even more on occasion, and weighing up to 12 or more pounds. The females are smaller and considerably lighter in weight. In coloration the true fisher somewhat resembles the silver fox. The general tone varies from brown to grayish brown, almost black on the back; pelage grayish tipped on the top of head and extending onto the shoulders; darker brown on throat, chest and belly; nose, feet and tail blackish.

The Pacific Fisher (*Martes pennanti pacifica*) originally ranged from southern British Columbia as far south as the northern part of California. This is the largest of the fishers and the largest of all the marten family to which it is closely related. Specimens of large males have been known to measure as much as 42 inches. The coloration of this variety is variable from dark yellow to blackish, generally lightest on head and shoulders and darkest on rump, tail and legs. Some pelts are almost entirely black. The *average* price brought by raw skins for all Canada in 1944 was $76.21.

The haunts of the fisher are quite similar to those preferred by the marten, although it has a modest liking to be close to a stream where fish can be caught. As its name signifies, it is adept at catching fish, although not nearly as skilled in the pursuit as the otter or even the mink.

As a hunter it is exceptionally expert, being one of the most powerful of all the smaller flesh-eating animals and by the other wild creatures upon which it preys.

Like the marten, it is as much at home in the tree-tops as on the ground, and it even captures and feeds upon the former when an occasion is presented. It is more nocturnal in its habits than the marten, rarely being seen in bright daylight. And like the wolverine, it has the habit of preying upon the other fur bearers which it happens to find caught in traps. But unlike the marten, it is particularly wary and difficult to trap.

In addition to all small mammals, birds, frogs, fish and some fruit and nuts, the fisher also regularly feeds upon the porcupine. It is one of the very few animals that does not hesitate to tackle the porcupine and is so skilled in this that it seldom suffers any unfortunate effects from such a conquest. It has a knack of turning the animated, big pin-cushions over on their backs to kill them; then literally eating them out of the shell. It has even been credited with killing bear cubs.

The young number from two to five to a litter, being born in early May throughout most of their range. The nest is generally in a hollow tree, although sometimes in a crevice of the rocks.

The fisher is both bold and shrewd. It has been reported to follow a trapper's trail and at each set which was visited carefully pull the set trap out of the way so that it could eat the bait without danger of being caught. Sometimes caught in a No. 1½ trap set for marten or other fur bearers, the fisher has been known to pull out without serious effects to itself. It has the strength of a small wolverine.

A No. 2 or No. 3 trap should be used for the fisher and the trap should be carefully concealed no matter what type of set is used.

These animals are inclined to follow regular routes in their quest for food and if the trapper can locate one of these routes his chances of catching the prize is generally good. The cubby can be used, as they seem to have little or no fear of going into them; but they are particularly smart in keeping out of a trap. Some trappers successfully outwit the fisher by placing two traps in the entrance to a cubby—one quite obvious and another to one side and skillfully hidden so that a suspicious fisher might think he was avoiding the really dangerous spot and step into the trap which was really intended to get him. A fairly large bait should be used, such as a whole rabbit, part of a porcupine, a grouse or even skunk. Fish oil and beaver castor are very helpful, as is also a mixture of anise oil, asafetida, muskrat musk and fish oil. The bait should be lightly covered with brush, etc., in the back of the cubby. Remember that the fisher is a good sized fur bearer, and the cubby should be about 24 inches high, 15 inches wide, and be topped over.

Natural holes in a bank, a suitably shaped crevice in rocks or a hollow log are also good places to make a baited set for fisher.

In all cases a drag should be used as the fisher will gnaw off his foot and pull out if the trap is staked or otherwise securely fastened.

FISHER

FORE

HIND

CUBBY SET

2½

BAIT

BURIED TRAP

EXPOSED TRAP

These animals (if ever you are fortunate enough to catch one!) should be skinned, cased and stretched fur side out. The feet and claws should be left on and the tail vertebrae pulled out without slitting the skin.

CHAPTER XVII

THE BADGER

THE badger is not considered a bonafide fur-bearing animal, although the hair of its hide is in considerable demand particularly by manufacturers of shaving brushes and artists' brushes and the price gained from prime skins generally justifies the effort in trapping this animal. During recent years prime northern badger pelts have brought the trapper a higher price than muskrat, raccoon, skunk or even black bear. Then, too, there is the nuisance value of trapping these animals, because of the extensive amount of holes and shallow burrows they dig in their quest for food and which proves so dangerous to riders in cattle country and destructive to crop lands.

There are four recognized varieties of the American badger:

The Common Badger (*Taxidea taxus taxus*) is found over a rather large area from Michigan to the Rocky Mountains and from central Manitoba, Saskatchewan and Alberta to southern Colorado and Kansas. This is the type variety. It is a large and particularly powerful member of the Weasel family, of which other related members are the wolverine, marten, skunks and otters. Its body is heavy; legs short and powerful; head comparatively small, broad and flat; tail short, thick and bushy; and pelage long and inclined to hang down on either side like an apron. In coloration the general appearance is silvery gray sprinkled with dark gray and black. This effect is produced by the individual hairs being grayish at the base, then a section of whitish, followed by a section of black and tipped with silvery white. Face black with a narrow whitish stripe running from the center of the forehead over the crest of the head to between the shoulders, and similarly colored patches on the cheeks circling outside the eyes, on the ears and sometimes on sides of head. The feet are black. Hair on head shorter than elsewhere. Belly whitish to yellowish. The males and females are about the same size; a mature animal measuring around 28 inches in total length and weighing up to about 23 pounds.

The Colorado Badger (*Taxidea taxus phippsi*) is found in southern California. It is larger than the Common Badger and generally with more black on face.

The Western or California Badger (*Taxidea taxus neglecta*) is found from California northward through Washington. The pelage has more dark brown instead of black; white head stripe sometimes runs to rump; belly buffy; tail light brown on top, paler underneath.

The Texas Badger (*Taxidea taxus berlandieri*) is found in the western half of Texas westward into southeastern California. All over coloration more yellowish and white head stripe running down center of back sometimes as far as base of tail.

The badger is primarily a creature of the plains, prairies and rolling areas, restricting its habitat to regions where the ground permits easy and extensive digging. According to official reports on areas within the United States, the greatest number of skins are taken in the State of Minnesota where the latest figures give 2,511 for the trapping season; North Dakota, 1,682; Wisconsin, 1,604; Nebraska, 1,516. Canada produces considerably more, with 6,183; Alberta, 4,031; and Manitoba, 957.

The principal food of the badger consists of small mammals such as ground squirrels, gophers, prairie-dogs, mice, etc., as well as an occasional seasonal meal of ground-nesting birds' eggs. In moving about on top the ground the badger is almost as slow and cumbersome as the porcupine; but when it comes to digging out its quarry, these creatures are quite remarkable. Instead of running-down its food, as most carnivorous or flesh-eating animals,

BADGER

LEFT HIND

LEFT FORE

4"

BURROW SET

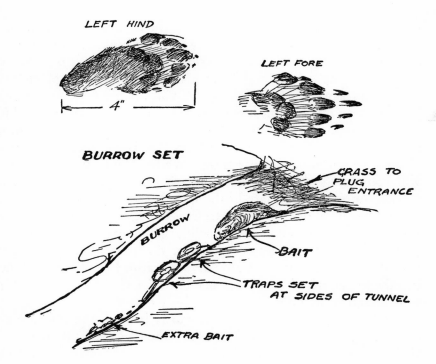

GRASS TO PLUG ENTRANCE

BURROW

BAIT

TRAPS SET AT SIDES OF TUNNEL

EXTRA BAIT

the badger pursues them almost entirely by digging. In fact, a large part of their time, throughout their life time, is spent by digging from place to place beneath the surface of the ground. To watch a badger start at the surface entrance to a ground squirrel's hole and proceed with digging to capture him, is a sight to be remembered. But if you approach, even most cautiously, the digger is pretty sure to hear the approach of your footsteps and the digging process instantly goes into high-gear, sending the earth flying as if propelled by a fast-moving mechanical device. It is surprising in what a short length of time badgers will dig out a whole colony of prairie dogs or other ground burrowing victims. And the mass of open holes and underground burrows which they will leave as a result is ample to cause strong language as well as serious concern to any rancher or farmer. These have probably caused more riders to go tumbling over their horses' heads, and more saddle horses' broken legs, than any other cause.

The badger has been termed "timid" by many writers, although such a term hardly does justice to these slow-moving underground-living creatures. Any one who has found a big badger far enough away from his burrow to bring him to bay, well knows how vicious he can be and what a fight he can put up. He will tear the average dog to shreds and ribbons, if the dog has the poor judgment to close in on him, and they are one of the most difficult of animals to kill. Blows that kill most any ordinary animal have but little effect on the badger. But if he gets only half-a chance, he will start digging most anywhere he happens to be and will completely disappear in a remarkably short length of time.

The young are born late in the spring, from May to early June, and the litter ranges from two to five. In regions where the winter is severe and the ground freezes solid, the badgers go into hibernation. The hair on the pelts is best for commercial use in winter. Probably far more of these animals are trapped or otherwise killed merely to get rid of their presence than for the sale of their skins —although what poor judgement this seems to be!

It takes a No. 3 trap to hold the sturdy badger, and they are not easily caught. Some trappers consider them as difficult to trap as the fox; and trap-wise old badgers have been known to dig out one trap after another, carefully turn it upside down and spring it, before proceeding to devour the bait which has been placed to entice it to be caught. Another trick of these animals is to cover so much earth over a set trap that it can be walked over without danger.

As the badger spends so much of its time underground the most successful place to set a trap is at the entrance to its den. This is made somewhat more difficult by the fact the badger does not have any large mound of loose earth at the entrance. He leaves it largely piled up behind him as he digs himself in, and then digs himself out. To make a set, remove this loose earth "plugging" as far down as you can reach. Conceal one or two traps down inside the hole. Set them at the sides, because the badger's feet are wide-spread. Scatter some pieces of bait beyond the traps, where they can be picked up and eaten before he comes to the traps. Then stake down a prairie dog, ground squirrel or even a rabbit, well above the traps; and finally fill the entire hole with dry grass. The traps should be slightly sunken and lightly covered with earth.

Some trappers make a fake set of a small trap which is left uncovered on top the ground inside a den hole. Another larger trap is concealed closer to the bait. The badger will upset or cover the small trap and thinking he has eliminated all the danger, walk into the trap which is really intended to catch him.

The dirt hole set used to catch foxes is also fairly effective in trapping badgers.

Although most badger trapping is done at the entrance to the animal's own den, they can be taken in baited sets made within areas where they are particularly active. Put a strong smelling bait inside the hole or a gopher, ground squirrel or prairie dog, and set the trap in the mound of earth close to the entrance—a little to one side where the badger's foot will step.

In cold weather, when the ground is frozen or the earth is solid, badgers can be "drowned out" of their holes—although this requires plenty of water close at hand and something of a bucket brigade to produce the desired results.

Badger skins should be skinned open and stretched as nearly square as possible. The tail should be split and stretched flat for drying.

CHAPTER XVIII

THE WOLVERINE

OF ALL THE animals native to North America the wolverine is probably the most genuinely hated by Indian and white trapper alike. To many he is unfavorably referred to as "Indian devil," "glutton" and "skunk-bear"; and his capture often provides a greater personal satisfaction than the reward derived from the sale of his pelt. Like the badger, to whom he is closely related, the value of his skin is not because of any demand on the part of fashionable fur manufacturers, but there are other good and valid uses for which it is highly prized. Its most important use is as trimming for the hoods of *parkas* worn by Eskimos and white men in extremely cold northern climates—because the fur is less apt than any other to "frost" from human breath. These skins bring a higher price among the natives along the Arctic coast than the best price to be collected in New York City. In many respects, the wolverine is more shrewd and more difficult to trap than the fox.

The Wolverine (*Gulo luscus* and related forms) is found intermittently and rather sparsely throughout most of North America from the northern tier of our States northward to the Arctic Ocean. Within this area there are three scientifically recognized varieties:

The Common Wolverine (*Gulo luscus*) ranges across the continent from Maine to Washington and northward to the Arctic Ocean. It is today extremely scarce, however, in most sections of the southern part of this range, where it once was to be found— as an indication of which, Michigan is officially referred to as the "Wolverine State." The Common Wolverine, which is the type variety, is a short and sturdy legged, powerfully built, bear-like animal with long, coarse hair. The males are slightly larger than the females and a full-grown male will have a total measurement of up to about 42 inches in total length and weigh as much as 35 pounds or more. The general coloration is dark brown, marked with a broad, pale brownish to yellowish white band which runs from each shoulder along each side of back to the rump where they merge and extend back onto the top of the tail about half way to the tip. This light coloring sometimes extends out over the top of the head almost to the eyes, generally becoming somewhat grizzled gray and brown; and also well down on both front and back legs. The somewhat elliptical dark brown area on the center of the back, the face and lower part of the legs and feet are rich dark brown. The throat generally is sparingly spotted with lemon yellow or whitish, very much as found in the martens to which the wolverine is also closely related. The belly is generally light brown.

The Southern Wolverine (*Gulo luteus*) ranges (or once did) through the mountainous regions of California northward through the coastal ranges into Alaska. It is considerably paler in general coloration than the type variety and somewhat smaller in size.

The Mount McKinley Wolverine (*Gulo hylaeus*) is a questionable variety found in the vicinity of Mount McKinley, Alaska. It is large in size and very dark in coloration, with a blackish tail.

Some naturalists believe that all of the wolverines in North America are of but one species and the slight regional variations are not sufficient to justify dividing into separate sub-divisions; while other scientists add four to six varieties in addition to the three above described. The reason for all this is the fact that the wolverine is, as a whole, one of the least known of all our fur-bearing animals. The habits and life history of even the rare sea otter are better known and understood by scientists than those of the wolverine.

Because of his unusual strength and stamina, the wolverine has through the centuries ceased to depend upon running down his game for food. His favorite method of procuring a feast is to find where other flesh-eating animals have made a kill and take it over for himself. Even the largest and most bad-mannered of the northern wolves give way before the bold aggressiveness of these fur-bearing highjackers; and it is claimed they will even drive a good sized black bear away from a fresh kill. Their particularly keen sense of smell also helps them to find the *caches* of other animals who have carefully hidden what they were unable to eat and have hidden for future meals.

Not only is the wolverine a highwayman and a thief, but there is an even worse side to his unsavory personality. Being a member of that large family, the *Mustelide,* to which the martens, weasels and skunks also belong, the wolverine is equipped with scent glands equally odoriferous to those of the skunks; and while he cannot spout his stench nor finds it necessary to use this as a means of self-protection, he uses the highly obnoxious fluid in a far more despicable manner. For after he has eaten all his abnormally large stomach can possibly hold, he deposits his stench all over what is left of the food so that no other animal that roams the wilds will touch it, no matter how hungry he may be. But this does not interfere with the wolverine returning and eating it with relish. This uncouth habit is also generally carried out when a wolverine breaks into the cabin or food *cache* of humans. It is a sad situation when a trapper, prospector or frontier settler comes home and finds that his own home or precious food supply has been visited by one of these animals.

To the trapper the wolverine is always a real menace. When one of the animals strikes the tracks or snow-shoe trail of a trapper through the northern wilds, it generally follows to find where the traps are set. If they are baited, the wolverine will cleverly upset and sometimes harmlessly spring the traps themselves and then eat the bait which has been left there. If there is a marten, mink or other valuable fur bearer already caught in the trap, the wolverine will tear it to pieces, eat the flesh and often leave his obnoxious stench as an added disgusting and insulting reminder to the trapper that he had been there. Then he will generally

WOLVERINE

FORE

HIND

5"

TRAP BURIED IN YOUR SNOWSHOE TRAIL

PLACE YOUR TRAP ON A PLATFORM MADE OF STICKS BEFORE YOU COVER IT WITH SNOW

SIX INCHES BENEATH THE SURFACE IS ABOUT RIGHT

follow the human tracks to the next set and repeat the performance.

They also destroy a considerable amount of valuable fur-bearing animals during the spring after the young are born. They seem to be particularly fond of young foxes. Finding a fox den which its keen nose tells him contains a litter of young ones, the wolverine will dig his way in to the nest and destroy the whole family. As an indication of their strength and persistence, they have been known to tear large areas of loose rock apart and the greater part of piles of driftwood nearly twenty-five yards in diameter to get to the nest or *cache* of another animal.

Their own nests are generally within some rocky cavern or at the end of a short burrow, made comfortable by dry leaves and grass; they have from two to five at a litter, born in June to early July; and they do not hibernate or store up food for bad weather.

Trapping the wolverine is often quite a problem. They are very difficult to catch and equally difficult to hold in a trap. But any time a trapper finds that one of these creatures is operating in his district, the best thing he can do is devote considerable effort to catching him (or them) or suffer the sad consequences throughout the season. Some trappers claim that a dead-fall set in front of a baited and trap-set cubby is an excellent method—as the wolverine seems more inclined to walk over the log and trip-stick of a wooden dead fall than he is to step into a steel trap. It takes a No. 3 or a No. 4 trap to hold him.

Probably the best method of taking the wolverine is to imitate the *cache* of another animal, by placing the carcass of a muskrat, beaver or most any other local animal, or head of a deer, in some recess among the rocks or a log pile, and cover it with grass, leaves, small brush, etc. Then very carefully set two to four or five traps in places where you think they may do the work for which they are intended. It is best to fasten the bait securely with a wire, so that even though the wolverine avoids or upsets most of the traps he may get into one trying to get the bait loose. Beaver castor scent added to the bait or close to it is an advantage.

Another method is to make a set right in your own snow-shoe trail. Dig down in the snow and bury a bait, or better scatter chopped pieces of strong smelling meat in the bottom of the snow hole, about a foot beneath the surface. Scatter some scent over it. Cover with sufficient snow to make a bed for your traps. Place the traps on a few pieces of stick to give them something of a platform to rest on; cover the pan with waxed paper or a cut pad as used in coyote trapping; and then fill the hole with snow level with the surface and lightly make the imprint of a snow-shoe on top. Drop some small bits of bait and some scent on top of the snow over the set—and hope that Mr. Wolverine will stop to dig out the bait.

It is well to remember that the wolverine prefers its meat a bit "high." If their stomach happens to be full, they generally will not feed on freshly killed meat—although they may despoil it with their obnoxious urine or excrement, and return in the next day or so to have a feed. So if you find your bait merely thus despoiled, be content and do not disturb the set, for the varmint may soon return. If they cannot eat all of the bait they may carry it away, if they can, and make a *cache* of their own. If such is found to be the case, and they have avoided or upset the traps, follow their tracks to the new *cache* and set two or three traps there. They are not generally so suspicious in approaching *caches* made by themselves. If they cannot dislodge the bait and carry it away, however, they may dislodge the trap or traps and carry these away—so that, upon their return, they will not be bothered with the traps' presence. If such is found to be the case, more carefully than before set another trap or traps—and keep your fingers crossed!

The traps must be securely staked or fastened to a heavy drag, as trapped wolverines have been known to pull a sizable log for several miles.

So, if you find a wolverine inhabits your trap line, you had better get busy and catch him; and if you want to get the best price for the skin, don't send it to the Big City for sale, but to some frontier town in the Far North.

Wolverine skins should be cased; the tail split; and it is best to leave the claws on.

CHAPTER XIX

THE MOUNTAIN LION

THE Mountain Lion (*Felis cougar* and related forms) is known by more different names than any other American game animal. It is frequently also called Cougar, Puma, Panther, Painter or Catamount. It was formerly found over practically all of North America as far north as the Great Lakes and northern British Columbia. Today, stories occasionally get into the newspapers to the effect that one of these big cats is believed to be roaming the woods of one of the middle-eastern States; but it is fairly certain that they are now extinct in most of their former range. However, they were for years claimed to be entirely extinct in the Florida Everglades.

There are eight different varieties of mountain lions found in North America. Their present range is exceedingly scattered and spotty. There are possibly a very few left in the Adirondacks, and the big swamps of Louisiana and Georgia, as well as in the Florida Everglades and the mountains of western America from Mexico to British Columbia.

Mountain lions are among the most wary and furtive of all our larger animals. A lion may spend years in a given area inhabited by a considerable number of human beings, and yet never permit itself to be seen by a single person. To still hunt them, without good dogs, is almost impossible. They are the ghosts of the wilds.

COUGAR

4"

FORE

HIND

X = HIDDEN TRAPS

The mountain lion is distinctly a killer—of everything from porcupines and skunks to elk and practically all varieties of domestic stock, especially the young.

The principal means employed in taking mountain lions is by the use of trained hounds. The use of poisons is not recommended, for it is unsafe to expose poisons on ranges where hunting dogs are being used. Under certain conditions mountain lions can easily be caught in Nos. 14 and 4½ Newhouse Traps.

Either of the traps recommended may be set on a known route of the mountain lion, preferably at a point where the route narrows. The animal generally has well-defined crossing points where it passes from one watershed to another in its search for food. Many of these are in the low saddles of divides, and at such crossings it is not uncommon to find "scratch hills," heaped up by the mountain lion in covering its urine. They are sometimes three to four inches high and four to six inches in diameter.

The mountain lion is trapped as it comes through the saddle of the divide and stops to visit a scratch hill, being attracted either by the hill itself or by a catnip lure placed there, as described later.

When the carcass of a domestic animal, deer, or other prey shows unmistakably that a mountain lion did the killing, at least three traps should be set around it; each 15 to 20 inches away. When the carcass is found lying on its side, one trap should be set between the fore and hind legs; another near the rump; and a third near the back and parallel with the loin. These traps require no lure other than the carcass. Frequently it is well to set a fourth trap six to eight feet away, if tracks show the exact route taken by the lion in approaching or leaving the carcass.

Why catnip is so attractive to members of the feline family is not yet fully known. Experiments have indicated that it has a soothing effect on the nervous system, similar to that of opiates on man. In some of the larger circuses, catnip has been used for years in gentling animals of the cat family. The use of catnip oil to lure members of this family within trapping distance has been remarkably effective. Pure catnip oil should be used diluted with pure petrolatum, 40 drops of the catnip oil to 2 ounces of petrolatum.

The hole for the trap set should be dug about 15 to 20 inches from a carcass, a single undisturbed scratch hill, or a tree on which a scent station has been placed; or directly in a trail where it narrows naturally or is made to narrow by rocks, brush, or other obstructions placed at the sides. The hole should be only slightly larger than the trap, and just deep enough to hold the set at a level slightly lower than the surrounding ground, with the drag and chain buried beneath it. The drag, which should preferably be of ½-inch wrought iron, should be attached to one end of the chain by a figure-8 swivel and it should end in two well-curved prongs. Bedding the drag under the trap, of course, requires more excavation. The drag chain should be at least eight feet long and attached to the base of the trap or to one of the springs.

At scratch hills it is well to place a trap on either side, the springs at right angles to the direction of travel. Experiments have proved that most of the larger predators, and particularly the mountain lion, tend to avoid stepping directly on any hard objects in a path. Knowing this tendency, the trapper may place a stick or a stone between the two traps and another at each approach.

After the trap has been firmly bedded it should be covered with earth and the surroundings left in a condition as nearly natural as possible. Dry horse or cow manure, finely pulverized, may be used to cover the inside of the trap jaws. Extreme care should be taken to keep all dirt from under the trap pan and to see that the open space there is at least one-fourth inch deep. The trap pan should be covered by a pad made of canvas or old descented slicker cloth, and cut to fit snugly inside the jaws; and all should then be covered, with finely pulverized earth, leaving the immediate area looking, as nearly as possible, as it did before the trap was buried. Leaving the ground over the trap in a perfectly natural condition, so that it blends with the surrounding area, is an art that requires much practice. Be sure to use a strong trap. Newhouse numbers 5, 15, 50 and 150 will do the job—they are designed for holding the biggest cats.

CHAPTER XX

THE BLACK BEAR

THE Black Bear (*Euarctos americanus* and related forms) is the biggest game the average trapper in North America can reasonably expect to catch. There are very few sections where the Grizzly (*Ursus horribilis* and related forms) are found, although there are probably more of these big bears today than there were twenty years ago, as a result of the protection they have received in the several National Parks. But the black bear has been much more successful in surviving in his native haunts and is today found in varying numbers over a considerable part of his original range, which included most of the wooded parts of North America from Alaska to the southern end of Florida and from Ungava to Mexico.

There are ten varieties of the black bears in North America; American, New Mexico, Kenai, Dall Island, Queen Charlotte, Olympic, Florida and Louisiana Black Bears; and the two color phases, Glacier or Blue and Kermode or White (Black) Bears. The "brown" and "cinnamon" bears are not distinct varieties.

The black bears are omnivorous in their feeding habits. They will eat most anything from an ant to a whale, grass to honey, acorns, berries, fish, roots, sheep, pigs, etc., etc.—whether it's fresh or carrion.

In some States the black bear is considered a game animal and

BLACK BEAR

FORE

8"

HIND

PEN SET

3 ft

BAIT

BURIED TRAP

is given protection by game laws, and promiscuous trapping of them is prohibited. In other States they are considered a predatory animal with no restrictions on their killing.

In most every area where these animals are numerous, certain individuals acquire much the same predatory habits which make the coyote, wolf and mountain lion often a scourge to the farmer or stock raiser. And when a bear once acquires the stock killing habit, there is only one way to cure him—kill him.

The most practical method of controlling the predatory bear is the intelligent use of the No. 5 or No. 15 Newhouse Bear Trap. The smaller No. 50 or 150 Trap will hold an average sized bear, but as the stock killing bear is nearly always an adult male of large size, the larger and stronger trap is recommended.

The sheep killing bear will stalk the flock when bedded down for the night. He will rush in and strike down a sheep, kill it and drag it into the brush or to some secluded spot. After he has gorged himself, he will usually make some effort to cover or hide the carcass, which is a sure sign that he will return for another meal.

In order to catch the animal under the above conditions it is necessary to build a V shaped enclosure at or near where the carcass was left. This enclosure should be built of substantial poles, and nailed or fastened together at the rear or narrow end. The carcass or a substantial portion of it should be placed in the rear or narrow end of the pen, and the trap set in the center of the open end.

Secure a green hardwood pole five inches in diameter at the small end and 7 or 8 feet long; drive the ring of the trap chain down over the small end of the pole as far as it will go; and drive several 20D spikes into the pole and bend them over the ring. In other words, make it absolutely impossible for the bear to lose this drag. If he does, you will lose your trap as well as the bear.

When the trap is set in the center of the open end of the pen, place a small pole across the pen about 3 or 4 inches higher and 8 or 10 inches in front of the trap. Stick dry dead sticks in the ground on both sides of the trap. The idea is to leave no place for the bear to set his foot except directly on the trap. The bear will not step on the pole or on the sticks you have stuck in the ground, but will have to step over the pole to get at the bait. If the structure is built of green poles, rub moist earth over all new cuttings; gather up all chips and cover everything with leaves and woods litter. Pull up some bracken or weeds and plant them around the structure. Try to make it all look natural and as though it had all been there a long time. All this should be done with great care, because if you pinch his toes and lose him, he will not stop killing sheep, but will be very difficult to trap.

When trapping for bears, particular caution should always carefully be taken to avoid the possibility of any human being, deer or domestic stock stepping into the big trap, and always carry a gun with which to kill your predatory bear.

No trapper, regardless of experience, should ever attempt to set a bear trap with improvised equipment such as a pole used as a lever. A setting clamp, with a single screw mechanism, is provided with each trap, together with a small auxiliary clamp for holding one spring while the other is being worked upon—and it is well to leave these in place until the trap is placed in position. After all, bear traps are darned powerful things and to have one accidentally snap closed on any part of your body, when you're a long ways from nowhere, does not come under the head of amusement!

CHAPTER XXI

THE CARE OF PELTS

HUNDREDS of thousands of dollars are lost to trappers annually because pelts are improperly skinned, fleshed, stretched, and dried. This is a great economic loss, not only to the trapping fraternity but to the raw fur trade and can be prevented if trappers would exercise greater care in selecting equipment and would learn the correct technique of skinning and preparing pelts.

Wilderness trappers usually whip off the pelts of captured fur bearers on the trap line, or on the spot, so to speak. The pelts are rolled or wrapped and carried back to camp for the finishing touches.

Trappers in settled areas usually maintain comparatively short trapping lines and travel back and forth, either by foot, horse-back, canoe or automobile. These trappers sometimes bring the animal carcass back home for skinning.

In either event most trappers maintain a headquarters camp and can procure or make proper pelting and finishing equipment.

Pelt drying boards.—First in importance is an ample supply of properly made drying boards. Too much emphasis cannot be placed on the vital need for providing the proper sizes and shapes of pelt drying boards, or, as they are commonly called, stretching boards. Unfortunately the word "stretching" is too often taken literally by trappers and stretching boards are s-t-r-e-t-c-h-i-n-g boards in fact. Boards that are out of proportion or skins that are stretched out of proportion always result in misshapen pelts. These are an eyesore and are materially disqualified by the raw fur buyer. Your goods are on display when you show them to the buyer, and otherwise good pelts are certainly shown at a disadvantage if improperly dried. They not only lack trimness but if overstretched invariably show up natural thin spots that should be pinched and covered with underfur and guard fur.

Most trappers prefer to make their own drying boards and here is where the skill and workmanship of the individual trapper comes into play. Drying boards should be smooth and as finished as possible. It is just as easy to make a thing right as it is to make it in a slip-shod fashion and this axiom certainly applies to trapper's equipment. Many trappers use formed wire or cut steel stretchers. Good results can be obtained by proper care both in selecting the right size and keeping the edges free from corrosion or rust. If this is not watched carefully, damaged pelts will result. Fine furs, such as mink, fox, etc., should be handled only on wood drying boards.

Skinning knives and appliances.—The trapper's prime requisite for the actual work of pelting is a good trapper's knife. The right kind of knife is equipped with a slitting blade, a skinning blade, and a small blade for general use. Each blade should be kept keen and sharp. A dull blade will cause more damage to pelts than a sharp blade that does its work smoothly and without friction.

Small, medium and large fleshing boards should be provided. These are best made of 2- by 8-inch material, 4 feet long and tapered from 8 inches at the upper end to 2 inches. Smaller sizes can be provided for animals smaller than a fox. The upper side should be slightly rounded to fit the curve in the fleshing knife.

The fleshing knife has a large, curved knife edge with a handle on each side. The edge should be dull so as not to cut the pelt. If preferred, a complete set of fleshing instruments can be made, or secured, of wood.

Another appliance that comes in handy is a tail slit guide. The manufactured guides are metal troughs tapered to fit the tail. An old umbrella rib also makes a good tail slit guide. A tablespoon is also handy for scraping and removing excess fat.

In addition the trapper should also provide himself with a tack hammer and tacks and split sticks for removing tail bones, a pair of nippers for cutting toes, and plenty of clean hardwood sawdust to absorb fat and dirt and give a good gripping surface on the pelt.

The stretched open or open-handled method is used almost universally for beaver, badger, raccoon, bear and wild cat, although some fur buyers prefer to have the full-furred northern type of coon cased. Open skins are taken off by cutting the skin straight down the belly, from the lower jaw to the vent, then slitting the front and hind legs to the body cut, after which the skin is carefully removed from carcass.

The case-handled method is used for such furs as wolf, fox, coyote, marten, fisher, mink, otter, lynx, skunk, opossum, muskrat, ermine, and civet cat. Cased skins are taken off by cutting down the back of the hind legs to the vent and then peeling the skin off carefully toward the head.

Care must be taken to keep the skin as free from flesh as possible. Use a sharp knife but guard against cutting into the skin. Peel the skin from the front legs, cut the ears close to the head and use great care in skinning around the eyes, nose, and mouth.

Feet and tails.—It is the customary practice to cut the tails off the muskrat, beaver and opossum. The feet should be cut off the following animals: muskrat, beaver, opossum, skunk, raccoon, badger, civet cat, and coyote. The feet of the other animals, should be left on and properly skinned and dried.

Fleshing.—There are certain mineral elements in fresh blood that tend to stain fur so it is advisable to wipe blood from the pelt as soon as possible, after skinning.

Fleshing is one of the most important operations in preparing the pelt. It is not only essential that all surplus flesh be removed but as much fat as possible. The layers of fat and muscle can be worked loose with the thumbnail and sawdust.

Place the pelt over the fleshing board and work down with the knife, using plenty of sawdust. Be careful not to scrape too hard. Overscraping will result in cutting the hair roots and cause the hair to fall out. Work the fat off carefully around the ears. If this is not done, the fat will very likely burn the fur and cause it to slip. Every trapper should accumulate a supply of hardwood sawdust. Use this freely when scraping off the fat.

Sawdust not only absorbs fat and grease but makes it possible to keep a firm grip on the slippery pelt. Sawdust can also be rubbed into the fur and then shaken out. By this means much of the dirt and grease can be eliminated from the fur and gives it a fresh, sparkling appearance. Never use salt or alum on fur pelts.

Placing the pelt on the drying board.—Select a proper sized board for each pelt. Your supply should include appropriate sizes to accommodate various sized pelts. When fitting the pelt to the board, be sure the belly is on one side of the board and the back on the other. Slip the pelt onto the board gently and don't stretch it but pull it down to full length and tack. A pelt that shrinks a little on the board is better than one that is stretched a little. Fleshed pelts dry quickly so it is important that they be placed on drying boards as soon as possible. Just before hanging the board straighten out the ears, tail, and legs.

Drying the pelt.—Drying is also an important process in the preparation of the pelt. Pelts should not be allowed to freeze nor should they be hung in a heated room. They should never hang where exposed to the sun. Pick a dry, dark space, keep flies away, and, if possible, provide for a circulation of air.

A small number of skins can be hung from nails in rafters or ceiling. If a large number of skins are to be dried, a frame can be made of 2 by 4 's or small, split logs. This frame slanted against a wall and studded with nails will hold a large number of skins. It is advisable to inspect the legs of pelts occasionally and make sure that they are drying properly. If tails and legs are not hanging straight, they should be pinned down. Pelts of foxes and other animals that are to be shipped "fur out" should be dried leather side out in a comparatively warm place for 24 hours then the pelt should be turned fur side out.

After drying, pelts should be removed from the boards and be given a final cleaning. Wipe the grease off pelts leather side out and if fur side out proceed as follows: Lay the pelt out on a clean table or bench and rub the fur full of clean hardwood sawdust. Be sure and rub sawdust in gently otherwise the guard hairs will be damaged.

Rub the fur until the grease is cleaned out. Shake the pelt out well and hang in a well-ventilated place. Skins should never be washed, nor should alum, salt or other preparations be used.

Packing and shipping.—Many dollars are lost to trappers annually because of improper packing. Green furs or furs that have not been stretched and dried should never be shipped. Skins should be properly packed in cloth or burlap and they should be laid leather side against leather side or fur side against fur side. Fine furs should be wrapped individually in absorbent paper or cloth before being packed into the bundle. Do not wrap in newspaper or any printed paper. The ink is apt to color pelts.

Pack the skins flat and sew bundles tight. Make the package big enough so the skins can be laid out, otherwise they will come out of the bundle all rolled up and creased and their full beauty will be lost. Your pelts will look much more valuable to the fur grader if they come out of the bundle flat and free from creases or rolling.

If you are selling your furs to the local buyer, take them to him or show them to him unpacked, as it is almost impossible to pack furs in a bundle and have them come out after shipping in as good an appearance as they were before being packed. In shipping furs, be sure to have your name and address both on the inside and outside of the package.

CHAPTER XXII

HINTS AND KINKS FOR OUTDOORSMEN

Siwashing at Zero

THERE is an old expression in the Northwest: "to go siwashing." Siwash is the name of a tribe of Indians in British Columbia. In years past they were exceptionally good woodsmen and hunters. They were, and still are, capable of getting along in the northern wilderness with very little or no equipment, even though the ground is deep with snow and the temperature is far below zero. Any expert woodsmen should be able to do the same— for some day it might mean the difference between life and death.

A man who really knows how to take care of himself in the wilds can live satisfactorily for days or even weeks, even in the Alaskan woods, without a single blanket or piece of canvas for a shelter. The only essentials are matches and a good heavy hunting knife or small axe. It is possible even without these, but dry matches are the most important to have with you.

Food and shelter are the bare requirements of existence. As for food, there are but very few wooded sections of the North where one cannot find porcupine—which can easily be killed with a stick. (The alternative is to build dead-falls for rabbits or larger game.) Even porcupine can be roasted over a fire in the open coals—quills and all. If you have no salt, roast some of your meat in the blaze of the fire until it is burned good and black. That helps.

As for shelter, and if you can find no natural open cave or over-hang of a rocky ledge in front of which to build your night-fire, it is quite easy to build a lean-to or spruce tree shelter. If you can find two big spruce trees growing side by side and with limbs that are thick and come clear to the ground, that is ideal. If they are on a slight angle, it is perfect. It will be dry underneath. Cut away the limbs on the down-hill side, so that it makes a "cave." Cut the limbs high enough that your fire will not ignite those over-hanging it. Build up around the sides and back with other spruce limbs. Make a back-log to reflect the heat of your fire inside. Do not make a bed of boughs. It is warmer to sleep on the bare dry ground. If you keep the fire going all night, you will be comfort-able.

If you build a lean-to, try to do so under some trees where the ground is free of snow. Otherwise you will have to build a bed of boughs. That permits cold air to circulate underneath, but is better than lying on the snow or damp ground. A ridge pole sup-ported by two trees or a tripod, is the first step in building a lean-to. Then lay other poles slanting against the ridge pole and cover with boughs. It is not as warm as a tree shelter, but is better than nothing. In any event, build a back-log to reflect the heat of your night-fire into whatever shelter you build.

Waterproof Matches

Matches can be of more importance than any other item in all your equipment, and wet matches are worse than no matches at all. If you go through the ice or otherwise get wet at low tempera-ture far from camp, a single dry match may save your life. Every person who travels in the so-called wilds in winter should carry a waterproof match container full of matches which are kept in exclusive reserve for an emergency. The screw top metal con-tainers are all right, but some people prefer the wooden ones. The matches carried in these containers do not have to be water-proofed, although it is an extra precaution to waterproof all the matches you carry. To do so, get a can of good shellac. When you want to use it, thin the shellac with alcohol—not too thin—and dip household matches in it. Dip them clear to the butt end. They can be stuck in a bar of soap or in the ground to dry. If the shellac is too thick, they will not burn well. But matches prepared in this simple manner can lie in water for hours and still ignite and burn well. A good makeshift match safe can be made out of a bottle, although this is apt to be broken in your pocket.

Frost-Bite

The best treatment for frost-bite or frozen parts of one's body is to thaw them out. In the case of frost-bitten hands, when on the trail, stick them inside your clothing next to the body. If it is your ears or nose, hold your bare hands over them, and rub to restore the circulation. If it is your feet, and no warm cabin is available, it may save you a lot of pain and inconvenience to stop and build a fire. But never rub snow on any frost-bitten part of your body. Why this idea ever found acceptance is a mystery—because rubbing snow on cold hands or feet will produce frost-bite rather than relieve it. The best treatment of all is *prevention*.

If you are wearing a parka with a fur-trimmed hood and have a beard on your face, and your breath causes the fur and beard to freeze together, do not attempt to pull the fur loose, because it is apt to peal off the outer skin from your face. This happens frequently in the North. Better hold your head near to a stove or fire until the frost melts.

Freezing to death is not an unpleasant way to get a ticket to the Happy Hunting Grounds—but it is always a one-way ticket! The surest symptoms are drowsiness. The snow always looks so soft and inviting—but don't believe it! Keep moving. Build a fire. If you can't build a fire, run a race with yourself. But don't sit down—the next thing you'll do is lie down—and that's the end!

The best way to cure frost-bite or freezing is to avoid it; and the best way to avoid it is to wear the right sort of clothing. If you are going to face really cold weather, do not skimp on good warm clothing. Wool is of course the only fabric—real wool. As for underwear, some experts prefer wearing two medium weight suits in preference to one heavy suit. But in any event, get good stuff.

The same applies to mackinaw shirts and pants. It is not always the garment that is the heaviest in actual weight that is the warmest; and do not make the mistake of putting on so much clothing that it will tire you out to carry it. The type of climate has a lot to do with it, too. You can be colder in above-zero in a damp climate than you would be at 30 below-zero in a dry climate. A finely woven cloth parka, as a wind-breaker, is excellent. A fur parka, for low temperatures, is better. Fall-killed young caribou skins make one of the warmest fur garments. Double-thickness rabbit skins quilted between blankets, make one of the warmest sleeping bags.

Feet are very important. If there is any chance of getting your feet wet, shoe pacs with rubber bottoms and leather tops are good —but be sure to get them large enough for at least two pairs of good heavy wool sox. And always wear fresh sox. Wash your sox frequently. At least hang them up over the stove each night and wear different ones the next day.

If you frost-bite your feet you must afterward be even more careful. They will become frost-bitten more easily thereafter. If you are in a country where there are plenty of big snow-shoe rabbits, catch a couple with snares. Case skin them—like you would a mink or fox. Turn the green skins fur side in; tie a string around the neck and cut off the rest of the head. While the skins are still green, put a pair of medium weight sox on your feet. Then work the green rabbit skin on, carefully fitting it to your feet. Then put another pair of light woolen sox over the rabbit skin. Over this you can pull real heavy sox—fur *mukluks* are even better. The heat of your feet will cause the skins to dry to the shape of your feet. At night, when you take them off, slip both pairs of sox off at the same time, with the rabbit skin left between them. This is one of the warmest foot-wearings you can find—and a great protection to feet that have recently been frost-bitten.

Those people who perspire very easily and freely are more apt to become frost-bitten than those with a dry skin. Surplus fat is theoretically an advantage, although the best travelers in the north country are generally as lean as a hungry coyote. There is more to knowing how to take care of yourself, than there is to your weight on the scales. Warm clothes and common sense are vitally important to a successful trip in cold country.

Waterproofing a Tent

Here are two methods of waterproofing canvas or other fabric for a tent or sleeping bag. The first method is not only the easiest but the most practical. In case the fabric is to be laid on the ground or for any other purpose than a tent, the second formula should not be used. In either case, a closely woven fabric should be used and remember that cotton goods shrink considerably when first soaked.

(1) Get a gallon of good gasoline, a pound of paraffin and an old broom. Heat the paraffin until it melts and stir same into the gallon of gasoline. Spread the tent or fabric out flat on the ground or a floor. Dip the broom into the mixture and "paint" the fabric thinly but evenly. Let it dry for a few hours. Go over the fabric with a rag to wipe off the surplus grease, and you have a tent that will keep you dry for a long time. When the dressing wears off, repeat the process.

(2) Another recommended process requires two tubs or wash boilers big enough for the purpose. First, soak the tent overnight in plain water and hang up to dry. Then in one of the tubs dissolve alum in hot, soft-water, in the proportions of one-fourth pound of alum to the gallon of water—and be sure the water is soft. In the other tub dissolve, in the same proportions, the same amount of sugar of lead (lead acetate, which is a poison) in soft hot water. Let the solutions stand until clear. Then pour the sugar of lead solution into the alum solution. Let stand for about four hours or until the lead sulphate has precipitated. Pour off the clear liquid, leaving the dregs. Then slowly and thoroughly work the tent into the clear solution with the hands until every part is penetrated; and let soak overnight. In the morning, rinse well in clear water, stretch, and hang up to dry. When the directions are properly followed, the fabric will not only be rainproof but practically sparkproof as well; however, this process is not practical for a ground sheet or for fabric exposed to friction. When the

mineral deposit gradually washes out of the fabric, repeat the process.

Most Dangerous Game

Most authorities consider that the most dangerous of all the animals found in North America is a "mean" domestic bull!

Purified Stream Water

There is an old belief that the water of a running stream purifies itself within a distance of within a hundred feet—but this is not true. Certainly virulent germs travel for many miles and remain dangerous to human beings.

To Keep Red Bugs Off

A preparation made of an ounce or more of flowers of sulphur mixed with enough pure rubbing alcohol to make a thin paste will keep the red bugs or chiggers away. Rub it on your legs and body before going out. It can easily be washed off at night. Kerosene is a fair substitute.

Finding Boot Leaks

An easy way to find small leaks in rubber boots is to turn them inside out; when thoroughly dry, fill with water and hang up. The smallest leak will soon show up on the dry lining. Mark a circle around each damp spot with ink—and make the necessary repairs after all the leaks have been marked.

Ants in Your Food-Box

Fasten short legs to your food-box and set the legs in saucers or can-tops filled with water. Ants do not like to swim.

How to Use a Map

A map is only a printed piece of paper unless you know the correct compass directions. If your map does not have the points of the compass printed on it, put them on yourself before you go into the woods. Then, when you really need to use your map, establish true north by using your pocket compass (or your watch); turn your map until the true or magnetic north on it points in exactly the same direction as your compass. Thus properly oriented, you can make proper use of the map. Do not depend on the old theory that moss always grows on the north side of a tree—because this is not always the case.

Any Watch Is a Compass

If you want to use your watch as a compass it is quite easy. Hold the watch with the face upward. Hold a match or any small straight stick in an upright position at the outer edge of the face of the watch at the outer point of the hour hand. Then turn the watch until the shadow of the match stick, which is made by the sun, falls along the hour hand. This will cause the hour hand to point directly toward the sun. If the time of day is in the morning, South will lie half-way between the hour hand and 12—in the direction in which the hands of the watch are traveling. If it is afternoon, South will be half-way between the hour hand and 12 —in the opposite direction from which the hands are traveling. The sun will give you true north. If you have a map, this can be computed for more accurate directions; but the true north is generally sufficient to give you the bearings necessary to get out of a predicament. Remember, however, that if your watch is set on daylight saving time it is one hour fast.

Indian Stove

Dig a hole about two feet deep in the ground. Find some slabs of rock to line the sides and bottom. At least cover the bottom with rock. Let a hot fire burn in this hole for about an hour, so as to thoroughly heat the rocks and surrounding earth. There are now two ways to use this fire hole for cooking:

(1) Rapidly clean out the embers and ashes. Cover the rocks on the bottom with a layer of green clean leaves from any "sweet" tree such as the maple, basswood, wild grape, or with vegetable

tops. Then place the articles to be cooked on this bed of leaves. This can be anything from fish to fowl or potatoes. Cover the food with another layer of leaves; cover the leaves with a piece of damp canvas; cover the canvas with about two inches of earth; build a fire on top of this; and forget the whole matter for two to five hours.

(2) Instead of cleaning the hot embers out of the fire hole, put a covered pot or iron covered-kettle (containing the food) on the embers and completely cover it with more red hot embers from another fire. Then cover with damp earth; build a fire on top; and forget for two to six hours. A pot of beans and sow-belly, or meat stew, can be put in the fire hole in the morning; and when you come back to camp at night, your supper is ready.

Jerked Venison

Mix together the following: 3 lbs. salt; 4 tablespoonfuls all-spice; 5 tablespoonfuls of black pepper; and 4 tablespoonfuls of cinnamon. Cut the meat in strips not longer than 12 inches and not thicker than 2 inches nor wider than four inches. Remove all enveloping membrane, so the curing powder will come in contact with the raw, moist meat—which must be moist and fresh so the powder will readily adhere; but do not apply water. Rub the powder mixture well into every part of the surface and dust it on a bit. Then hang each piece of meat by a string and let it dry in a place where fresh air can get at it, but never hang in the sun, nor where it will get wet, nor too near to artificial heat. Meat thus prepared is not at its best for eating until it is about a month old and it does not require cooking.

Calling a Fox

If you can imitate the sound of a rabbit in distress, you can call a fox. The old-time Indian did this by sucking on the back of his hand.

The Big Buffalo Kill

The years 1872, 1873 and 1874 saw the greatest slaughter of the American buffalo. According to the Smithsonian Institute, of

Washington, D. C., at least 1,401,000 buffalo were killed during the single year of 1872. The estimate for the three years runs to more than 5,370,000. It was not only the greatest slaughter of game in all history, but the most regrettable.

Snake Bite

The bite of any snake is apt to be dangerous. Take no chances. There are only four really poisonous snakes in the United States. They are: the rattlesnake; the copperhead; the cotton-mouth moccasin; and the coral snake. The latter is a very pretty little devil found in the deep South, the least known of the four; and the most dangerous. To be bitten by any of these requires quick action and drastic action—if death is to be avoided. It is, however, consoling to know that about 85 per cent of the persons bitten by poisonous snakes survive. Like many other such circumstances, the best practice is to avoid being seriously involved. If you are traveling in country where poisonous snakes are found, wear high, heavy leather boots; and leather gloves when using your hands in suspicious places. If you happen to be bitten, tie a handerchief or other tourniquet around the arm or leg above the bite. But do not tie it too tightly and keep moving it up as the swelling progresses. Immediately make an incision in the flesh across each fang mark, like XX. These cuts should be about one-fourth inch deep and one-half inch long, or longer if it was a very large snake. Be sure that the blade is sterile. Holding over a flame will do this. Free bleeding helps. A little squeezing sometimes helps to start the flow of blood.

Then apply suction—with your own lips, if nothing else is available. If your teeth are in bad condition, or if you happen to have any open sores in your mouth, this is dangerous. Deaths have resulted from snake venom getting into a bad tooth cavity. In any event, quickly spit out; and wash your mouth thoroughly with clear water. A better suction can be gained by using a heated large-mouth bottle. Suction should be continued for at least half an hour and repeated for about 15 minutes at each succeeding hour. In the meantime, keep wet dressings on the wound to keep the wound open and the blood draining. Keep quiet—for exertion will

tend to spread the poison through your circulation. Get to medical
aid, if possible. Do not take alcoholic stimulants. If you are on
good terms with your Creator, you'll probably pull through.

Pemmican

There are a number of white man's recipes for making pemmican—including chocolate, raisins and what-not. But here is the
old-time Indian's method for making it: Take the required amount
of jerked meat and grind it finely. The Indian did this by pound-
ing between stones. Mix the ground jerkie with one-third part of
melted fat. To this can, if desired, be added any ground dried
fruit. The whole is then compressed into containers. If kept dry
it will keep for four or five years.

For variation, make the melted fat by boiling broken marrow
bones in water and skimming off the fat. Fish pemmican can be
made in the same manner by using ground dried fish instead of
meat.

Moth Prevention

If you have a trophy skin that you have tanned yourself or
which you want to make mothproof, here is a formula recommended by the National Museum, Washington, D. C.:

Boil two ounces of arsenic in one pint of water. Use a pail or can
of at least a quart capacity and one that you can afterward throw
away. After 15 minutes of boiling, let it cool to a point where
the container will not burn your hands; then add one pint of
denatured alcohol. Stir well and allow to settle.

Hold the skin upside down, so the liquid will run to the base
of the hairs, and apply the clear liquid with a piece of sponge on
a stick, or a small paint brush. The skin should be superficially wet,
but not soaked to a point where it will dry out of shape. If properly done, the skin should be mothproof for the rest of its natural
days.

As the arsenic solution is exceedingly poisonous (as well as in-
expensive) any surplus should be disposed of where it cannot be
reached by beast or man; and the can should be thoroughly rinsed

before being pounded out of shape and thrown away. The sponge or brush should be burned.

Ground Sheet

A good ground sheet is often a luxury as well as a necessity. Sleeping on damp ground is both unpleasant and detrimental to man as well as his blankets or sleeping bag. A rubber coated poncho is mighty nice; but you can make just as good a ground sheet, with very little trouble. To do so, take a piece of fairly heavy canvas (part of an old tent will do) and cut it to the desired size. If the added weight is no handicap, it is well to make it large enough to not only lay your sleeping bag or blankets upon, but so it can be folded over the top as well. Get several bars of paraffin or candles and rub these into the canvas—which has been laid out flat on the floor. The rough surface of the canvas will scrape off fine particles of the paraffin. Rub it into the fibre until the surface is colored white with it. Then use a warm iron (not too hot) and press the paraffin into the fabric. With care the canvas can be so filled with the paraffin that no moisture can come through. If the canvas is heavy, it may be necessary to repeat the operation on the opposite side.

Purifying Oil

Purified neat's-foot oil makes excellent gun oil. To purify, drop a few strips of lead or some shot into a bottle of the oil and place same in the sun's rays. A heavy deposit will take place, filling the lower part of the bottle. The other part becomes bright and limpid—which is the purified oil. Pour this in a separate bottle. A repetition of the process will thoroughly purify the oil. It is in this manner that watchmakers purify the oil used in lubricating their delicate machinery. Oil prepared from the fat of the ruffed grouse also makes good gun oil.

Tanning Skins

Any one can tan a skin. It just takes a little work. Following is how the plains Indians did it:

The fleshing process should be done soon after the skin is removed from the carcass, while it is still soft and moist. The hide can be staked out on the ground or held over a smooth log or even one's own knee; but scrape or cut off all the surplus fat and flesh. Do not cut so close that the ends of the hairs are sliced off.

If the hair is to be removed, this can be done by soaking in water to which ashes are added, or the hair can be scraped off with a sharp-edged tool.

Next comes the braining. The Indians made a preparation of boiled brains, liver, grease and pounded soaproot. (The soaproot and liver can be omitted.) Approximately the whole brain and liver of an animal is required to dress its hide. The mixture is rubbed into the skin. After this get a bundle of dry grass and lay this in the center of the skin; saturate the grass with hot water; fold the corners of the skin over this, in bag fashion; twist the skin tightly into a solid ball; tie it up; and hang to soak overnight.

Next comes the stripping. Open the hide and twist out all the water and moisture that you can. Then stretch on a frame and go to work on it with any instrument resembling a hoe. This causes the water to ooze out of the skin; and thus go over the entire skin until no moisture piles up ahead of the hoe. When fairly free of moisture, let the skin dry and bleach.

Then comes the working or softening process, which is the hardest work of all. This is done by drawing the hide for some time in a seesaw fashion over an upright smoothed edge of a board or the limb of a tree. Keep up this process until the skin is soft.

If the skin is to be smoked, a pit is first dug in the ground. A fire is then made in the pit and allowed to burn until a mass of hot ashes and glowing embers accumulates. Pieces of damp, rotten oak are then placed on the ashes, causing a dense smoke. The skin, being previously dressed as described, is stretched over the pit and allowed to remain in the smoke two or three hours.

Corned Meat

To add variety or difference to your wild meat menu, it can be very tastily corned. The following recipe is proportioned for about a six-pound chunk of solid meat—deer, elk, moose or just plain cow. Mix 4 tablespoons of sugar, 6 tablespoons of coarse salt and 1 tablespoon of pulverized saltpeter in 1 quart of cold water. Put the chunk of meat in a large kettle; pour over it—the above mixture; and add just enough water to cover the meat. Let this stand in a cool place for 48 hours, turning the meat several times during this time to insure even curing. At the end of the 48 hours remove the meat and boil it until tender, in fresh water. The cooking usually requires as much as three or four hours. It can be served either hot or cold.

Poison Ivy

Poisoning from poison ivy, poison oak or poison sumac can be far more annoying than disastrous. This like many other undesirable things, should be avoided rather than cured. The best first aid, however, is to wash the affected parts as soon as possible with ordinary yellow laundry soap and warm water. Rub the soap in vigorously, as though you meant it. This will often prevent further development or spreading. If the first aid treatment is given too late, and inflammation and water blisters develop, and if you can get to a drug store, get an ounce of "tincture of iron." Dilute this with 10 ounces of alcohol and 10 ounces of water. Paint it on the affected parts. If this preparation is not available, make a thick paste of laundry soap and water, which should be spread over the affected parts and left over-night.

Burns

One of the best simple remedies for a burn, whether mild or severe is baking soda (or epsom salts) mixed in cooled water which has been boiled. Put it on a gauze dressing or a clean white handkerchief or piece of cloth. The soda should be kept moist by applying just enough water to keep it well moist. Never use cotton on a burn, because it will stick to the wound.

Making Rawhide

You can make your own rawhide for shoe laces, thongs, snowshoe webbing, etc. There are several methods, but the following is simple as well as efficient. Soak the deer or other skin in water in which ashes (or lye) has been mixed. When the hair begins to slip, remove the hide and scrape off the hair. Stretch the hide tightly on a frame or wall, where the sun will not shine on it and it will not be rained upon. Rub into the skin any boot oil or animal fat. Allow the hide to dry. Then work it over the edge of a plank or narrow edge of a pole, until the skin is fairly pliable. Cut in strips to suit your needs.

Cooking Fish Ducks

As soon after killing as possible, cut open the skin down the center of the breast; peel the skin down the sides; and cut out the breasts. This contains most of the meat. Soak overnight in strong salt water. Wash in fresh water. Fry or broil with a strip of bacon laid over. They are not bad at all!

Fence Jumping Deer

Deer have been known to jump over an eight-foot high fence from a standing start, without so much as taking a preliminary step. It requires at least an eleven to twelve-foot fence to keep deer in or out. There are also records of their making broadjump leaps of thirty feet in length.

Wolf Weights

Large male timber wolves will tip the scales around 75 to 100 pounds; and exceptionally large individuals of the northern varieties found in Upper Canada and Alaska will go as heavy as 150 pounds and possibly even more.

Muskrat Meat

If you have never eaten muskrat, try it some time. Their feeding and living habits are about as clean as any animal or fowl you have ever served on your dinner table; and their flesh is very palatable. Cook them the same as you would a rabbit. It goes without saying that the two scent glands should be removed. They can easily be recognized as two slightly bluish glands under the skin on the belly between the hind legs.

Porcupine Quills

A dog with a face stuck full of porcupine quills is always a problem to his master; and the worst part of it is that most dogs will go back for a second dose, no matter how painful the first experience may be or how many times they have endured it. There is, however, a comparatively easy way to remove porcupine quills. You don't have to yank them out, as most people do. Most of the quills can be twisted out, just like a corkscrew. The sharp ends are covered with small barbs, which lie down when the point is jabbed into flesh, and open like dozens of harpoon heads when the quill is pulled back. But when the quill is twisted, these little barbs lie down against the body of the quill. The short stubby ones are a little more difficult; but most quills can be twisted out with your fingers.

Skins for Taxidermy

If you kill a deer or other antlered animal which, for any reason, you want to get to a taxidermist to have the head mounted, remove the cape by cutting the skins up the back of the neck. (Do not make the cut up the throat.) Before your incision reaches the base of the antlers, stop cutting and branch off to the back of each antler—so that the top of the incision forms a Y. Then skin out the head. If the skin is to be dried, it is best to remove the cartilage from the ears, and nose, and split the lips. If you have salt, however, it is better to salt the skin. After fleshing the skin carefully and well, rub the salt in thoroughly all over and roll up. To be safe, repeat the salting in a day or two—after removing all the surplus liquid which has accumulated. To be even safer, do this a third time.

The Rope Pack

A piece of rope about three-eighths inch in diameter and 15 to 18 feet long is a mighty handy item in the equipment of the hunter or trapper. It's a pretty good habit to keep such a piece of rope tied around your waist every time you go into the woods. You may carry it for a long time before you need it. But when you do need it, it will amply repay you for all the trouble; and if you have it, you will find many uses for it.

One good example of the use of a rope is the rope pack. Lay the rope on the ground. The two ends should be parallel and just far enough apart so that you can sit down between them. Then lay whatever you want to pack across the rope about midway between the two ends and the curved top. The pack can be anything from a sack of grub to a freshly killed rolled bear skin or a deer. Then sit down with your back to the pack and the ends of the rope extending downward beside your legs. Lean back against the pack, and reaching back over the pack pull the loop of the rope up over your head. Pull it pretty well down below your chin to the center of your chest. Then pick up an end of the rope in each hand and slipping each end under the loop of the rope which has been pulled over your head, cinch it down tight and tie it. By leaning backward against the pack and pulling the rope tighter, you can fasten your pack so that when you get to your feet it will be held securely well up on your back, where a pack belongs. By tying the ends of the rope with slip knots, the pack can be instantly dropped by pulling the loose ends, if emergency demands.

Martens for Pets

When caught young, Martens can be domesticated into really desirable house or cabin pets. They can be house-broken; and become as tame and playful as cats.

Campfire Barbecue

One of the easiest and most practical methods of cooking meat over a campfire is to roast it on a revolving wire and rope suspended from above. Fasten any large chunk of meat to a wire; attach the wire to a rope; and suspend same from the limb of a tree, or otherwise, over the fire. Wind it up and then let the meat rotate slowly at it cooks. A leg of venison cooked in this manner is hard to beat. It was a favorite method of cooking used by the Indians.

World's Record Beaver?

What trapper would not thrill at catching the biggest beaver on earth? A 60-pound beaver is a big beaver; but one of these grand fur bearers was trapped on December 2, 1938, by John Webster, of Tie Siding, in the Laramie Mountains just north of the Medicine Bow National Forest, Wyoming, that weighed 115 pounds with the skin on and 109 pounds after the skin was removed! Another beaver trapped out of the same colony weighed 91 pounds. The facts in the case are substantiated by the District Forest Ranger and the Wyoming Game and Fish Commission; and so far as records are available, this sets an unofficial world's record for beaver.

Possum and Sweet Potatoes

Here's a good way to cook that next possum you get . . . providing you can find some sweet potatoes to go with it. First boil the possum until partly done, in a strong sage tea. Then place in a roaster and sprinkle well with salt, black pepper and red pepper; and strip with fat salt pork. Add enough hot water to prevent burning and fill around with sliced sweet potatoes . . . and cook until done. Does it make your mouth water?

Flavored with Gall

Some persons have the belief that the gall, which is found attached to the liver of an animal, is poisonous. This is not true. In fact, one of the favorite dishes of the American Indians, before the days of tin cans, was "liver of buffalo sprinkled with gall." But, after all, the old-time Indians also considered the skunk as a desirable item in their menu. The meat of the latter is white; they are clean animals; and, if you like a skunk flavoring, a skunk stew is nothing to turn up your nose at. (Note: This is not a recommendation!)

Roast Beaver Tail

Jam the point of a stick into the base of a beaver tail, just as you might do with a frankfurter, and hold it over the hot coals of a campfire. It is not necessary to remove the skin, as this will "blister" and easily peel off as the roasting progresses. The meat is white and most people consider it very palatable.

Hot-Coals Roasting

Often the simplest methods produce the most satisfactory results. Fish or fowl cooked in the red hot coals of a campfire, without the use of any pot or pan, is sometimes an emergency necessity; but it produces as delectable a dish as any city chef can concoct in the fanciest fashionable kitchen. For example, take a sizable trout of three or four pounds, fresh from the cold stream. Cut only a small hole at the throat to remove the intestines. Wash the inside thoroughly and season with salt and pepper. If the makings are available, fill with a dressing made of dampened bread crumbs or broken crackers and chopped meat with a mixture of bits of bacon. Sew up the opening tightly. In the meantime you should have prepared your campfire so as to produce a good bed of red-hot coals. Make a pocket in these hot embers and lay your fish right in it—then carefully rake the coals over the fish and let it cook for half an hour or more, depending on the heat and the size of the fish. When the fish is removed, peel off the skin—and you have a dish fit for the most particular epicure. The fish can, if desired, be laid on a tin plate and covered with another, when put in the bed of coals.

Ducks, grouse and other wild fowl can be cooked in the same manner. Merely remove the intestines through as small a hole in the abdomen as possible. After washing out thoroughly, fill with dressing and sew up tightly. Then wet the feathers thoroughly (or cover them with clay or mud) and place the whole bird in a bed of red hot coals just as in the case of the fish; completely cover with the coals; and leave until done. An hour will generally be sufficient. When the bird is removed, peel off the feathers and skin—and you'll never forget that first meal cooked by this method.

Camp Johnnycake

Put the required amount of sifted corn meal in a basin or bucket; add a little salt; and pour on scalding hot water until you have mixed it into a stiff batter. Put this batter, a large spoonful at a time, into sizzling hot grease; turning it over and over until it is "done brown." The hot grease of venison, bacon or fish is swell. Serve hot, with sugar and butter. And with venison or fish to go with it—no man could ask more!

Insects Vamouse!

In many parts of the country where trappers live, insects are more than mere pests—they are hordes of pests. The average person can become so accustomed to mosquitoes that they cease to be a major problem; but there are very few men who can become accustomed to some of the other stinging insects. To clean out the insects from a tent or small cabin, one of the best methods is to burn Buack (an insect powder). Pour a little pile in a saucer or the lid of a tin and light. It burns and smokes like Chinese punk, and the fumes will kill insects like nobody's business.

A good lotion for outdoor use is: mix equal parts of common tar with sweet oil and rub same on face, neck, etc. Another lotion is: warm about three ounces of hog's lard and add half an ounce of oil of pennyroyal. Rub on in the same manner. There are also a number of patented preparations which will do the trick.

Leather Boot Soles

A good preparation for the soles of leather boots, to make them waterproof and add to their period of usefulness, is to make a mixture of mutton-tallow, bees-wax and rosin (proportions of about 5-4-2). When melted together, soak the bottoms of your boots in this warm mixture until the leather will not absorb any more.

Wolf Blood

Any person who has handled a dog team knows the value of having wolf blood in his animals. The work of a sled dog is mighty tough and there are exceedingly few breeds of dogs that can stand it. Their feet are usually the first part to give out. Icicles have a habit of forming on the long hairs between their eyes, which cause them to go lame. A man who follows a sled drawn by dogs should watch for the first signs of lameness among his team. It will generally first show up in a small spot of blood in the dog's tracks in the snow. The ice which collects between their toes causes the toes to swell and crack. If this is not caught soon enough the dog will become useless and have to be taken out of the team. Sometimes they even become unable to follow, and must be put on the sled. Most dog-mushers in the North carry little sacks or moccasins which can be tied on the dog's feet in such emergencies. With a moccasin on a dog's foot the animal has some difficulty in pulling its share of the load, but this is better than taking him out of the team.

The wolf is practically immune to this sort of lameness. Their feet are far tougher than those of domestic dogs. Added to this important asset is their unusual strength and stamina. This is why wolf blood in the veins of a sled dog is so desirable. The more wolf blood they possess, the meaner their disposition is apt to be—but sled dogs are not pets; they are work animals.

The wild wolf and the domestic dog will breed together. In the North, many sled dogs are allowed to run loose in the summer. This is particularly true of the dogs owned by Eskimos and Indians. In this way they occasionally fall heir to a litter of half-breed wolf pups—by natural course of events. It is also possible to tie out a domestic bitch when in heat. There is always the danger of the bitch being killed. It is also possible to raise captured wolf pups for breeding stock. But no matter how it gets there, wolf blood in your dog team will certainly give you more miles per gallon on a tough winter trail with your sled.